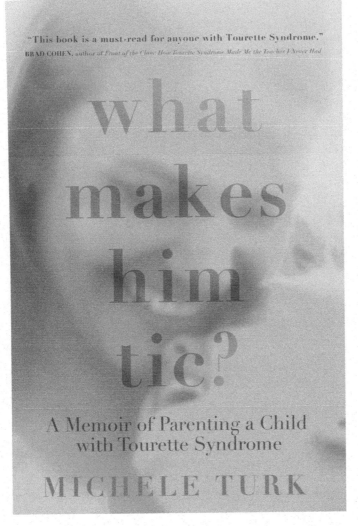

"This book is a must-read for anyone with Tourette Syndrome."
BRAD COHEN, author of *Front of the Class: How Tourette Syndrome Made Me the Teacher I Never Had*

what makes him tic?

A Memoir of Parenting a Child with Tourette Syndrome

MICHELE TURK

what makes him tic?

A Memoir of Parenting a Child with Tourette Syndrome

MICHELE TURK

woodhall press

Woodhall Press | Norwalk, CT

Woodhall Press, Norwalk, CT 06855
WoodhallPress.com

Cover design: Jessica Dionne
Layout artist: L.J. Mucci

Library of Congress Cataloging-in-Publication Data available
ISBN 978-1-954907-92-8   (paper: alk paper)
ISBN 978-1-954907-93-5   (electronic)

First Edition
Distributed by Independent Publishers Group
(800) 888-4741

Printed in the United States of America

This is a work of creative nonfiction. All of the events in this memoir are true to the best of the author's memory. Some names and identifying features have been changed to protect the identity of certain parties. The author in no way represents any company, corporation, or brand, mentioned herein.

To my mother, Marjorie Pullia, who taught me to count my blessings

"We owe it to people with Tourette syndrome to talk about what makes them tic. Michele Turk nails it as she gives the disease a voice and invites us to walk the road with her as well as share in the fascination, beauty, and sorrow that accompany a 'tic-ing' life."

—MICHAEL S. OKUN, M.D., Neurologist, executive director of the Norman Fixel Institute for Neurological Diseases at University of Florida Health, and author of *Tourette Syndrome: 10 Secrets to a Happier Life*

"Music has always been my escape from TS, as well as my gateway into living a 'normal' life with it. Raising a child with a neurodivergent cocktail of TS and Asperger's, my mom had limited resources and unimaginable obstacles. If only she'd had a firsthand account of another mother's journey. *What Makes Him Tic?* is one of those invaluable resources for parents that says, "You're not alone."

—JAMES DURBIN, Musician and *American Idol* finalist

Chapter 1

The Bitch in the House

"Bitch. Bitch. *Bitch!*"

I was in the kitchen cleaning up the Saturday morning breakfast dishes when I heard it for the first time. I turned off the faucet, put the dish towel on the island, and listened closely. More cursing. The words were loud and piercing, bouncing off the walls of our home.

I peeked around the corner. My 11-year-old son, Michael, was sitting on the couch, a rust-colored sectional my husband, Russ, and I had owned since the late '90s. My daughter, Katie, then 9, sat next to Michael watching *SpongeBob*. Katie had clearly heard the swear words but was ignoring Michael, aside from the occasional side-glance.

Michael looked as he always did on weekend mornings: in his flannel pajamas and T-shirt, his chestnut hair mushrooming atop his still boyish face. Then he cursed again, and there was no question about what he'd said: *bitch*. He said it again. And again.

I stared at him as if he had just spoken in tongues.

Michael glanced at me a few times as if he didn't know what was going on either. He didn't look upset, just a bit tense. I could tell he sensed my anxiety and confusion as I stood there in my sweatshirt and navy pajamas. "Michael...are you OK? Is something upsetting you? Are you angry?"

"I'm fine."

He continued to stare at the TV. Then he barked the words again, in a high-pitched staccato that sounded as if he were possessed.

"*Shit! Shit! Shit! Bitch! Bitch! Bitch!*"

By then, Russ had come into the living room, his eyebrows raised, forming a familiar furrow across his forehead. We watched our son spit out the verboten words and at the same time act as if it were any other Saturday morning.

"Are you saying these words on purpose?" I asked.

He said he wasn't. I wasn't sure I believed him.

Russ and I looked at each other, likely thinking the same thing— that Michael was acting out or trying to get attention, something he'd done since he was in preschool. But he didn't stop cursing, even when we tried to ignore the words, the way we had when he was a toddler throwing a tantrum. Ignoring him didn't work; after several minutes of silence, the cursing would start up again, sometimes so loud that Michael himself seemed startled, as if he had been awakened by his own snoring.

By the end of the day, which was the Saturday of Martin Luther King Jr. weekend in 2011, I was in full panic mode. I immediately suspected our son had Tourette syndrome. What else would cause a kid to curse uncontrollably? It was a classic sign, or so I thought.

My husband, a doctor specializing in obstetrics and gynecology, remained calm. He rarely got agitated or animated about any medical problem. And this one was at least a bit familiar. Michael had had mild motor tics—sudden, uncontrollable movements—since he was 7 years old, repeatedly blinking his eyes and occasionally grimacing. At first, the pediatrician diagnosed seasonal allergies, which was a relief. But when the tics continued year-round, we consulted several doctors and therapists who assured us that tics were quite common in boys and that our son would likely outgrow them. And indeed, the tics would come and go throughout elementary school, without becoming too frequent or significantly worse. Over the past month, however, I'd noticed that Michael had been mumbling sounds under his breath. But I dismissed it as a new tic that would likely go away as all the others had. After all, the experts had told us not to worry.

Worrying was in my genes. After rolling my eyes at my overprotective Italian-American parents for decades, I had become a world-class worrier myself. And hearing my son screaming obscenities in a barely human screech was like being awakened from a dream by a clap of thunder. At times, I actually jumped, as if someone had come up behind me and said, "Boo!"

Motioning Russ into the kitchen, I whispered, "Should we go to the ER?"

He tilted his head to the side and said, "That's probably not necessary yet."

"Right. It's not a medical emergency. What would we say—'Uh, my son won't stop cursing?'"

He nodded.

"Then what do we do?"

~

It was supposed to have been a relaxing holiday weekend—paging through the Sunday paper, putting the house in order a bit, and unpacking whatever boxes remained. We'd moved back into our home only a month earlier, after six months of living in a nearby rental during what turned out to be a major renovation. Basically, the contractors tore down our Cape Cod–style home, leaving only one room untouched—Katie's bedroom, which was now an office. For years we'd dreamed of turning our outdated, increasingly run-down house into a home where we would each have our own space. The rental was tiny for a family of four, and I had been hell-bent on getting into the new house by Christmas. The renovation was finally done, and we moved back in on December 17. The next day, we bought a Fraser fir, as usual, and put it in the living room corner, decorating the tree with the box of ornaments I had set aside months before.

The morning of Michael's outbursts, we had no real plans, in part because Russ was on call, meaning he might have to head to the hospital to deliver a baby at any time. That's why the rest of us were still in our pajamas and the kids were still watching TV; I'd relaxed my usual get-up-and-get-away-from-screens policy.

As Michael watched and cursed, cursed and watched, he remained almost preternaturally calm, which surprised me. I wondered if maybe he was relieved that he could finally let it all out. All day, I kept my gaze on him, watching and waiting, sometimes murmuring, "Don't worry" and "It will be all right." I'm not sure if I was trying to reassure him or myself, but either way, Michael turned a deaf ear to my comments. In truth, I was not sure it would be all right.

Russ and I sat down with Michael and asked him if he was saying these words on purpose. He denied it. Katie didn't believe him, and I was beginning to suspect that he was playing us a bit. To be honest, I didn't know what to think. *It had to be Tourette*, I thought. *But how could my son have Tourette?*

Just after lunchtime, I snuck away, closed my office door, and googled "Tourette's syndrome" (now more commonly referred to as

4

Tourette syndrome, or Tourette). I spent a good hour in my office as Michael's tics created an ambient echo throughout our house.

I learned that Tourette is a rare neurological disorder that affects an estimated one in 160 kids between the ages of 7 and 17 in the U.S., a number that has become a moving target. I also learned that Tourette is three times more common in boys than girls and less common in Hispanic and non-Hispanic Black people.

Even though symptoms can change in number, type, and severity over time, and wax and wane, it is a chronic condition, like diabetes. I was relieved to read that most kids with Tourette syndrome improve through their teen years, and some stop ticcing altogether by the time they reach adulthood. Others never improve.

When I typed "compulsive cursing," the word that popped up on the screen was *coprolalia,* defined as the uncontrollable urge to curse or use other offensive language. It surprised me to learn that this symptom was exceedingly rare, affecting only about 10% of children with Tourette despite being portrayed as commonplace. The U.S. Centers for Disease Control and Prevention (CDC) website summed it up well: "Probably the most common misbelief about Tourette, often seen on TV and in movies, is that people with the condition blurt out obscenities or curse words. The reality is that most people with Tourette do not excessively or uncontrollably use inappropriate language."

This tidbit was not reassuring—my son seemingly had a rare manifestation of a rare condition. By 5 p.m., I was more than ready for a glass of wine. I opened a bottle of red to go with the feta-filled chicken baking in the oven. We sat at our new island in the new kitchen of the almost-new house we had been dreaming about for nearly a decade. I don't remember what we discussed that night, but I do remember the awkward feeling of having an unwanted guest.

After dinner, the four of us settled on the couch pretending that Michael wasn't acting as if he were possessed. As we watched a movie, it felt like we were the ones doing the acting. By the time the credits were rolling, the bottle of wine was empty, but I was not chill.

~

When I think back to that day, I realize I'd never experienced anything quite so jarring. I had never been hospitalized, save for the two times I'd given birth. Russ was the picture of health. Michael had croup as an infant and later developed allergies and asthma, and Katie had a little trouble gaining weight as a toddler. But overall, we were a healthy lot. Until that day, when Michael said the word *bitch* at least 100 times and the word *shit* only slightly less often. And every time, it caught me off guard.

I wondered if stress was the culprit or played some role. After all, he had just started sixth grade and was now in middle school, in a new building with many new students. He complained a lot about not having friends, about the cool kids, the cocky football players. And he was just getting used to the "new" house, which still lacked rugs and art, every sound echoing through the still-mostly-bare rooms.

Russ had painted our new bedroom himself. The color, called Gray Cashmere, was soothing, placid. I wanted my bedroom to be a haven, like a country inn, and I loved the result, our walls lined with tiny bookshelves tucked into the eaves that flanked the new king-size bed my mother had given us for Christmas. But I couldn't relax.

That day, the day Michael began cursing, I tried to stay relatively calm—on the outside. But my long-held fear that something bad would happen to one of my kids had seemingly been realized. I was not just shocked, I was shell-shocked.

Katie, for her part, tried to ignore her brother even more than usual. Later, she said she was convinced Michael was cursing intentionally and thought he was getting away with something huge. As much as I suspected my son had a medical problem, I couldn't blame her for thinking that, especially when he looked his sister in the eye just before dinner and shouted, "*Bitch!*"

"Are you doing that on purpose?!" I asked again.

He looked directly at me. "*Bitch!*"

I knew then that he wasn't faking. He could be defiant, especially when he was younger, but he would never call me a bitch. He was only 11, for God's sake.

That night, as I was getting ready for bed, I heard a sound coming from Michael's room down the hall. Eavesdropping, I leaned my ear against the door and heard what I thought I had heard: My son had said a new word. One I hadn't realized he'd known. The N-word. When I opened his door, there was silence. Michael was sleeping in the same bed, under the same blue and gray plaid comforter, breathing rhythmic, peaceful breaths. As he lay there, motionless, his hair tousled, he looked like the picture of innocence. But he was a different boy, forever changed. *What made him choose a word that was not only forbidden in our home, but was the vilest, most hateful word I could think of?*

Back in my room, the N-word ringing in my ears, I lay next to Russ in our new bed, my mind fast-forwarding through the years at breakneck speed. *Will this continue forever? Will he be able to go to school, go to a supermarket or restaurant, get a job, get married?* I pictured my son living with us forever, holed up, too embarrassed to go out in public.

I opened my laptop and continued reading. I read that there is no cure for Tourette syndrome. Prescription medications are available to alleviate some symptoms, but pharmaceuticals work for only some people. I found no explanation for why kids with coprolalia said the words they did, but I did learn that it was not based on their beliefs or biases.

In between tears, I thanked God when I read that people with Tourette typically live full, long lives and that their intelligence isn't affected.

"At least it's not something worse," Russ said, trying to comfort me. I always tease him that he's a glass-half-full guy, whereas I'm more of a skeptic; it's in my nature as a journalist. This time, I had the same reaction.

"I know," I said. "I thought the same thing."

That was one of the last things we agreed on for a long time.

Chapter 2

The Good Mother

I never really trusted my instincts as a mother.

Until Michael was born when I was 34, I had never changed a diaper, burped or fed a baby.

But worrying that I didn't have what it took to care for an infant was only part of my fear, the other, perhaps more ominous, concern being that I just wasn't cut out for motherhood. I came by my fears honestly. My mother, despite having four kids in just over 10 years, worried about us constantly. After I, her second child, was born, my aunt and grandmother told my mother that she shouldn't have more kids because she was such a nervous Nellie. There were two more, plus a couple of miscarriages (my parents were devout Catholics).

Mom had always said, "I don't like babies." When she came to visit us in D.C. for a week after Michael was born, she cooked veal parmigiana and fettuccine Alfredo, did the laundry daily, and even washed the bath mats. But she refused to take care of Michael. True to form, the only time mom held Michael the whole week was to snap a photo before she left for home.

My father, who died in 2008, was even more of a worrier, if that was possible. His mother died of breast cancer at 34, when my father was 6 years old. He lived every day in fear that one of us would be taken from him too. "You kids are all I have," he would say. At the time, his words made us feel like a rare and precious species living among more common breeds. But my father's outlook added even more pressure; I wasn't sure I could love a child the way my parents loved me.

My parents—especially my mother—had strong opinions about what it meant to be a good mother, which influenced my approach to parenting. To my mind, motherhood meant cooking dinner every night, whether or not you liked to cook. It meant 51 weeks of hard work a year and one week of fun. On week 52, my parents hopped a plane to Puerto Rico with five other couples. So great was their fear that we would be orphaned that my mother and her sister never flew on the same flight; that way, if one plane went down, the surviving sister would raise the nieces and nephews. In other words, in my mind, motherhood meant sacrifice.

I grew up in an old-school small town in New Jersey deemed the most Italian town in the country in the 2010 census. My parents didn't pressure me to achieve, but faith in God and practicing Catholicism were commandments that didn't need to be etched in stone. Once my siblings and I became adults, my mother used to say, "If you kids don't go to church, I will have failed as a mother." What also went unspoken was the role of family in our lives. Sunday dinners, daily visits to my grandfather in his last years, birthdays with cousins, and weeknight dinners at 6 p.m. no matter what.

If our house was built on His rock, my mother was the one who kept it standing. When my mom wasn't feeding or taking care of us, she was volunteering in the school cafeteria or the hospital gift shop. She baked for us every week. And she baked for other people—a cheesecake every time someone died—and this went on for decades. I just didn't think I had the energy or wherewithal to put in what she had.

No wonder, then, when the time came to talk about having kids, I was ambivalent, to say the least. I didn't seem to have the yearning I saw in so many other women my age, which explained in part why Russ and I waited nine years—until he was 35 and I was 34. The whole time, I worried that someday, I *would* feel that yearning, but that by then it would be too late. I was also seriously afraid of screwing the whole thing up, just by the fact that I wanted to have a career, something my mother and mother-in-law never had after they had children.

One day, just before Russ and I were married, my mother and mother-in-law, both stay-at-home mothers, were chatting in our kitchen. I remember one of them saying, "All of the women I know who work have no choice." The other agreed. Then my mother turned to me. At the time, I was working for the Red Cross, coordinating volunteers to lend a hand in disasters. "I think you should be a volunteer," she said sweetly. I ignored them, albeit politely, but my mother still held a lot of sway over me, and knowing she would disapprove if I had a career was upsetting.

Russ and I talked—and joked—about our decision to put off having kids. But given his demanding schedule as a doctor, we both knew the heavy lifting would fall on me, so he didn't pressure me. Then, seven years into our marriage, I came to the realization that though I wasn't enthusiastic about having kids, I didn't want a life without them, either. Russ was nervous but relieved. Given his profession, he was a bit concerned that if we waited too long, we might have to deal with infertility. And so we began "trying."

~

I had managed to live for 32 years as one kind of person—carefree and calm, at least on the outside. I was the student who, in college, waited until the last minute to write my papers or cram for tests, staying up all night to complete assignments but rarely skipping a night out with friends, even if it meant nodding off on a barstool, which I did more than once. After graduation, I took off to Los Angeles to work as a full-time volunteer in a homeless shelter through a program called the Jesuit Volunteer Corps. Afterward, I moved back East, ostensibly because it was my dream to live in New York City. But that's also where Russ was attending medical school.

A few years later, Russ and I got married. I was 25 and he was 26. We moved into a one-bedroom apartment in Manhattan, where we stayed for the four years Russ worked as a medical resident in the Bronx. When we weren't working, we went to bars and restaurants with friends, jogged and Rollerbladed in Central Park, and enjoyed the city. Then we moved to Washington, D.C., because we had a lot of friends there and Russ was looking for a more manageable city than New York after he finished his training. Our social life became even more jam-packed, and we also traveled a fair amount, from annual trips to the beach with family or college friends to a few "before the kids arrive" trips abroad.

That all changed when I got pregnant with Michael. Before this one, I'd had a miscarriage at 10 weeks. During my routine ultrasound, I looked at the screen but didn't know what to look for. Then I glanced at Russ, whose face had turned the color of concrete. I could not see what he saw, but I knew it was not good. We weren't going to have this baby.

Losing a pregnancy made me want to be pregnant. I think that setback made both of us realize that we were not only ready but really wanted to become parents. I got pregnant again nine months later.

That's when I morphed into my worrywart praying-for-a-healthy-baby mother and my four-pack-a-day father all rolled into one (although I never smoked). When I was carrying Michael, I obsessed over everything I ate and tracked my daily food intake, weight, and exercise in a journal. I surfed the Internet and read a half-dozen books about pregnancy and childbirth, which only fed my insecurities. One night, I became frantic after eating cantaloupe that had been sliced on the same cutting board as a piece of raw meat, which, in turn, may have been infected with listeria, which can cause miscarriages. I'd spent a decade listening to my husband recount worst-case scenarios in otherwise healthy women like me, which only fueled my fears.

As my due date approached, I worried not only about the delivery but also about leaving the hospital with an infant in my arms. Even before my kids were born, I felt I had to protect them, the same way my parents protected me. This animal-like instinct was exhausting. It felt like sleeping with the lights on all night. Russ was much calmer, which, rather than comforting me, made me feel as if I carried the burden for both of us.

Two years before I had Michael, I published an essay in *The Washington Post* titled "Motherhood Angst," chronicling my myriad fears about becoming a mother. I explained in detail that as a medical reporter and wife of an ob-gyn, childbirth was demystified, but being discharged from the hospital, tot in tow, terrified me. As long as you had a car seat for your infant, newly minted parents just strolled out of the hospital and drove off. *What would I do next? Where was the owner's manual?* Talk about on-the-job training! I knew, with a sinking feeling, that I wasn't up to the task. There were so many minute decisions—how to burp and diaper a baby, and what to do when colic kicks in—and I was afraid of making a fatal mistake.

The essay only scratched the surface. Until I had a child, I had never feared failure. But once I became a mother, fear—which must have been there all along, courtesy of my DNA—took over like a weed, nearly choking me for two decades.

It's not that I lacked confidence. It's just that I was all too aware of my strengths and weaknesses. I'm very good at throwing a party. When I was younger, I was really good at bar games—shooting pool, throwing darts, and pinball, probably due to my uncanny hand-eye coordination. I have a reputation for being funny, in part because not having a sense of humor was akin to being an atheist in my family. I can bake an array of goodies. I am a good reporter and a decent writer, friend, wife, and daughter. I have what Russ calls a "strong moral compass," developed from the sense of right and wrong instilled in me by my parents and extended family. I am empathetic to a fault. And I'm loyal—unless I feel betrayed. But let's not go there just yet.

Yet I also knew that in my heart, I had been something of a slacker, doing just the minimum required to get by because that last-minute approach had always worked for me. I have a tendency to be scattered and disorganized. My office is stuffed with so many papers and magazines that if I stacked everything up, the pile would reach the ceiling. This was not going to cut it when it came to parenting a child. Plus, I can be selfish, self-righteous, and stubborn. I harbor resentments and hold a grudge, an undesirable trait that would rear its head a few times in the coming years.

I fell in love with baby Michael the moment I saw him, the shocking mass of black hair matted to his head, his flushed complexion, even the blood mixed with white pasty gunk that covered his writhing body.

I thought he was perfect, and I never again questioned whether I should have had a child. Those very early days were exhausting but also blissful. As tired as I was with his every-two-hours nursing schedule, I relished every little change as Michael's personality took shape. But as our son survived his first days, weeks, and months with us, the angst returned. I fretted that my baby was jaundiced, that he would choke on his food, drown in the pool, run into the street, that I would die and leave him orphaned.... Like father, like daughter, I guess. It's as if I knew something big was going to go down, and I was prepping for it.

Chapter 3

I Have Tourette,
But Tourette Doesn't Have Me

On the Tuesday after Martin Luther King Jr. weekend, I put Katie on the bus, called Michael's school to say he would be out sick, then drove him to the pediatrician, a doctor who had been taking care of him since he was a year old. But instead of getting out of the car and walking inside as we usually did, I pulled into the parking lot and called the office number.

"Hi, this is Michael's mom. We're here," I told the receptionist.

I'd warned her about Michael's cursing beforehand, so when we got inside, she whisked us into an exam room, then shut the door. Michael sat on the table, his pudgy belly hanging over his boxer shorts. When the doctor came in, I didn't have to explain Michael's

16

symptoms. On cue, he blurted out the usual staccato, *Bitch. Bitch. Bitch. Shit. Shit. Shit.*

She didn't even flinch. I'd always liked this pediatrician because she didn't sweat the small stuff but was decisive in emergencies. After some small talk, she began her interrogation. "Has he had strep recently?" she asked, flipping through his chart.

I shook my head. I had read that PANDAS (pediatric autoimmune neuropsychiatric disorders associated with streptococcus) is sometimes blamed for the sudden onset of Tourette-like symptoms in the weeks after an infection with streptococcus bacteria, but Michael hadn't had strep in recent months.

"Any other recent illnesses?"

The only thing I could remember was a cold back in October.

She continued with her questions, about recent illnesses and other symptoms, but the appointment felt a bit perfunctory. She said she needed to rule out several disorders that could cause ticcing, but she didn't give us a diagnosis. Instead, she gave us a prescription to get bloodwork done, and a note to explain Michael's absence from school. Then she told us to call a pediatric neurologist, naming the same one Michael had seen a few years before, who'd told us his tics were nothing to worry about.

As with many neurological conditions, there is no test for Tourette. Doctors come to a diagnosis after assessing a patient's history and observing their symptoms. "Do you think it's Tourette syndrome?" I asked. "I mean, what else could it be?" In the past few days, I had typed Michael's symptoms into the computer again and again, looking for other conditions that might mimic Tourette. As much as I didn't want Michael to have Tourette syndrome, I also worried that it could be something even worse, like a brain tumor, even though I knew that was unlikely.

The doctor said it was too soon to tell what was going on, which disappointed me. I wasn't expecting a definitive answer, but I'd hoped for, well, *some* morsel of information to hang on to. As soon as we got home, I called the neurologist and took the next available appointment, which was a week away. Given Michael's near-constant cursing, that felt like an eternity. I remember thinking, *What am I going to do at home with him for a week?*

I decided I needed to ramp up my research. I figured that if I combined my investigative skills as a journalist with Russ's 20 years of medical expertise, we could pinpoint why the tics had come on so suddenly—and find the smoking gun that had caused them. I racked my brain, reaching for any recent ailments, infections, or odd exposures that could be causing my son to do this. That, I hoped, would lead me to the magic bullet that would make everything go back to normal. Never mind that scientists with actual training and experience had been trying to find a single cause and cure for Tourette for more than a century.

French neurologist Georges Gilles de la Tourette is credited with discovering Tourette in 1885. He published a landmark study of nine patients who had what he referred to as *maladie des tics*. At the time, Tourette was considered a strange psychiatric disorder, an enigma akin to hysteria—a syndrome Gilles de la Tourette had also studied. Scientists no longer view it that way, but as one medical study summed it up, "[Tourette] has long rested in the shadowy borderland between neurology and psychiatry."

For many decades, there wasn't much research devoted to Tourette, at least compared with other neurological illnesses. In fact, the Tourette Association of America (TAA) was not founded until the 1970s (back then it was known as the National Tourette Syndrome Association). When I started probing, visiting the TAA website over and over, I realized I knew pretty much what most people knew—or thought they knew—about Tourette syndrome, which was oftentimes inaccurate information gleaned from TV shows and pop culture. In other words, I assumed, as many people do, that Tourette was all about cursing. There was a memorable scene from Season 3 of the show *Curb Your Enthusiasm*, where Larry David hires a chef with Tourette syndrome for his new restaurant in Los Angeles. During the grand opening, the chef, who is cooking in an open kitchen, begins shouting a string of obscenities. Fearing that the patrons will leave, Larry also begins cursing to cover it up. Soon, all the diners chime in with profanities of their own, which leads everybody to laugh and raise their glasses.

If only it were that simple.

In my research, I came across a video of a 2006 interview on *The Oprah Winfrey Show* with Brad Cohen, author of *Front of the Class: How Tourette Syndrome Made Me the Teacher I Never Had*. In the clip, he tells Oprah how his fifth-grade teacher made him stand up in front of the class and apologize for making noises, and promise it would not happen again. He also recounted how his mother was approached by a woman in the grocery store who asked if her son was "possessed by the devil." This was exactly why my first impulse was to keep Michael out of school.

"The media in our country have done a tremendous disservice to individuals with Tourette in the way it's portrayed," Dr. Keith Coffman, a neurologist who is co-chair of the TAA's medical advisory board, told me. "It's still very stigmatizing, which is why there are people who say, 'No, it's not Tourette, it has to be something else, it can't be Tourette.'"

It also doesn't help that a lot of the information surrounding Tourette is fluid. Even the name of the condition has changed several times over the years—it has been called Tourette's syndrome, Tourette syndrome, Tourette disorder, and simply Tourette. The definition of the condition has also changed. In the *Diagnostic and Statistical Manual of Mental Disorders (DSM)*, a comprehensive reference book that classifies mental conditions, Tourette was first labeled a psychiatric disorder, then a neuropsychiatric disorder. In the most recent version, the *DSM-5-TR*, published in 2013, it is called a neurodevelopmental disorder.

No wonder Tourette is sometimes called the most misunderstood well-known condition.

During that first week after the start of Michael's symptoms, as we waited for our appointment with the neurologist, I'd sit in bed with a stack of literature spread on top of our new paisley comforter. The colors were meant to be soothing, like everything else I'd picked for our refurbished bedroom. Yet instead of drifting off, I spent hours in bed reading studies and familiarizing myself with a whole new vocabulary, including *echolalia* (when you repeat another person's words) and *stereotypies* (movements like head banging or arm flapping). Michael had neither of these symptoms.

When I am researching a story, my strategy has always been to read everything I can, find prominent experts, and see where that leads me. I love doing research, and in the old pre-Internet days, I'd lose myself for hours looking through microfilm at the library. Characteristically, within a week of Michael's first swear word, I'd amassed a dossier of information: the aforementioned studies, plus brochures from the Tourette Association and lists of specialists.

As much as I hoped that what Michael had was just a phase, or, as the medical literature put it, a "transient" or "provisional" tic disorder that would resolve on its own, I had to admit he had a lot of the telltale symptoms of Tourette. In fact, his progression seemed classic: His tics had begun when he was 7, increased in frequency and severity between ages 8 and 11 or so, and were now peaking as he approached his 12th birthday, in four months. One statistic that gave me a glimmer of hope was that roughly one-third of kids completely outgrew Tourette by the time they became young adults; one-third experienced at least some improvement; and only a third continued to tic into adulthood.

I also learned that people with Tourette often have co-occurring conditions such as ADHD and obsessive-compulsive disorder (OCD).

At one of the lectures I would later attend, the speaker showed a Venn diagram showing Tourette, OCD, and ADHD, explaining that all kids with Tourette have some of each. "It's not whether you have the other symptoms, but how much," he said.

In fact, Tourette typically presents with a constellation of symptoms, including ADHD, as well as behavioral problems, anxiety, learning disabilities, depression, and autism spectrum disorder. The whole cluster is sometimes called "Tourette Plus."

An image kept popping up in my Internet searches—that of the tip of an iceberg jutting out of the water with the words *motor tics* and *vocal tics* written on it. But beneath the water, on the submerged part of the iceberg, were 17 additional words and phrases, including *rage, behavioral issues, learning disabilities, anxiety,* and *ADHD*. The caption reads: *Tics are just the tip of the iceberg.*

Michael had never been diagnosed with any of these conditions, but he had exhibited some ADHD and OCD traits. Later, he told me that the nagging urge to swear felt akin to OCD in that "something just needs to be done a certain way or else you won't feel quite right."

The only person I'd ever met with Tourette was a professor I'd had in journalism school. His symptoms were obvious—verbal tics that seemed more like a stammer. He announced to the class on the first day that he had Tourette, which became clear because of the sounds that occasionally interrupted his lectures. Yet he stood up in front of our classroom of young adults and lectured brilliantly and cogently. The memory of this professor also gave me hope.

After Michael began ticcing, I started to notice people ticcing everywhere I went: the cashier at our local supermarket, an old friend, a college tour guide. Even President Obama developed an eye twitch soon after taking office. That's not surprising since stress can make tics worse.

Yet the causes of Tourette are still somewhat mysterious. Nearly everything I found online said that Tourette was hereditary, but that environmental factors also played a role and could exacerbate the underlying condition. I learned that Tourette is a dominant gene and that parents have a 50/50 chance of passing the gene on to their children. This nugget really throws a lot of parents for a loop as they think back through their family tree and assign blame to every quirky relative.

This seeming contradiction got my wheels spinning. Like most families, we did not know of anyone with Tourette, but Russ and I—and our extended families—certainly had some lively discussions about which side of the family had more comorbidities like OCD or anxiety, and we were able to identify one relative with a minor motor tic (eye blinking).

The blame game comes as no surprise to most Tourette experts. Dr. James Leckman, a child psychiatrist who served as the Director of Research for the Yale Child Study Center for more than two decades, recounted his experience over the years meeting with families for the first time. "In some of the patients I've seen, I'll be doing an evaluation and I ask the parents if there is anybody else with tics besides their child, and they say 'no,'" he recalled recently. "But if you actually look at the individual who is telling you that, they are ticcing away."

According to a book I picked up early on, *A Family's Guide to Tourette Syndrome*, kids who develop Tourette must have multiple risk factors. "It is only when multiple risk genes [exist] (perhaps being contributed from both sides of the family) that sufficient risk to develop the disorder occurs," the authors write. And "there are some experts who believe that this genetic risk must be 'activated' by some sort of environmental cause, like conditions developed in utero or during childbirth, or an infection."

One aspect I didn't find much information on was the impact Tourette can have on families. I hadn't really thought of that until the night Russ, Katie, and I all watched a video called *I Have Tourette's But Tourette's Doesn't Have Me*, put out by the TAA. In it, a bunch of kids about Michael's age explain their condition, all while squeaking, shaking, jerking their heads, coughing, grunting, twitching, snapping their fingers, sniffing, and flapping their arms. None of them cursed, at least not on-screen.

The video was hard enough to watch, but what stayed with me is Katie's reaction. As soon as the credits rolled, she hopped over the arm of the couch and bolted upstairs to her bedroom, where she proceeded to pull the covers over her head and burst into tears.

Naturally, I ran after her.

"Why are you crying? What's wrong?" I asked, gently peeling off the blanket.

She said she felt bad that she had yelled at Michael to stop cursing.

"I've been a bad sister," she said. "I was mean to him."

I had been so focused on Michael that I hadn't thought about what my 9-year-old was making of all this. I tried to explain that we all felt overwhelmed and confused, that I didn't know what to make of it and neither did her dad. I assured her that she was a good girl even though she felt irritated by Michael's outbursts sometimes. Katie and Michael had been almost inseparable since she was born; they even slept in the same bedroom for a few years, with Michael on the top bunk and Katie on the bottom, because she was afraid to sleep alone in her room. Now, her older brother must have seemed foreign and frightening. That night, my heart broke for her.

I knew that one more thing on my to-do list was to keep Katie, a sweet and smart kid who was doing very well in school, on track. What I didn't consider was the emotional impact this crisis would have on Russ and me. That came later.

Chapter 4

The Journalist and the Doctor

In the 11 years since Michael was born, Russ had relied on me to take the lead parenting role, which seemed fair, given that I was working part-time from home and he had a demanding job.

Still, I expected that Russ would show more interest in the treasure trove of information I was uncovering in my nightly research. To be clear, it's not as if we didn't talk about Tourette and Michael. And Russ was also willing to indulge me as I shared various factoids from my pile of studies, books, and pamphlets. But after working 70- to 80-hour weeks, including a couple of 24-hour shifts on the labor and delivery floor every month, he was pooped. I got that, but it also irritated me. *Is he in denial?* I wondered, looking over at him reading a novel, as if he didn't have a care in the world. After all, I knew he could be incredibly focused, organized, and driven when

24

he wanted to be. His roommates in college called him "the great monomaniac." And when he was chief resident at a hospital in the Bronx, his colleagues nicknamed him Russolini.

I wanted him to feel the urgency, angst, and agita I felt. *I* couldn't stop and read a novel. *I* couldn't relax, despite the nightly glass—or two—of wine. One week after Tourette invaded our world, he was reading a freaking novel!

"Are you just going to sit there and read your book?" I finally snapped, a few days before Michael's appointment with the neurologist. "We need to *do* something!" I whisper-shouted, surprising both of us when I grabbed my stack of papers, flinging them at him. "Jesus Christ, *I'm* not the one who went to medical school."

He looked at me, startled. Then, to his credit, he put aside the novel, read the studies, then summarized them for me in a flat tone, explaining that it was likely that Michael had Tourette and that he would probably need some medication. Russ also said that it was early, and we needed to see what the neurologist said. He didn't feel comfortable digging through the literature, trying to make predictions. "I'm a gynecologist," he said. "I'm not going to pretend I know everything about Tourette after reading a few articles. Let's wait and see."

Later, he told me that his professors had spent "five minutes" covering Tourette in medical school. *Fair enough,* I thought. Plus, I knew that Russ had seen his share of family tragedies in his line of work, including stillbirths. But this was his own kid, for God's sake. *Show some emotion!*

The first time I heard Russ talking to a patient at length, I did a double take. We were in our bedroom, he was on the phone, and he was speaking in a tone I had never heard before in all our years together, a voice so soothing, so slow, low, and singsongy that I instantly realized he was talking to an anxious mother-to-be.

That was the voice I wanted now, the one I hoped Michael and I would hear, the soothing Dr. Turk with the reassuring bedside manner, whose years of dealing with babies and new mothers could calm this mother and our baby.

I also wanted my husband's help and expertise, instead of being the only one researching, taking notes, and making phone calls. I wanted him to be as fired up as I was. Looking back, I realize I wanted something he had never been able to give me: his undivided attention.

At the time, I didn't try to see my husband's side of the story. A decade earlier, Russ had left a good job in D.C. that he loved and where they loved him back, promoting him and offering him a raise to stay, because I wanted to move back to the New York area. The practice he joined in Connecticut was not all that he had hoped for. His partner traveled three months out of the year, leaving Russ behind to deliver the babies. When the guy officially reneged on their contract to make Russ a partner, Russ opened his own practice. At 40, Russ essentially had to start over, taking on a lot of debt for office renovations and equipment, and then launching and running a medical office on top of being a doctor. It also initiated a rocky period in our marriage and our lives.

He was stressed, and rightly so. But I needed him. *We* needed him. And so, angry, frustrated, and feeling very alone, I shut off the light, turned my back to my husband, and tried to sleep. And the next morning, I made only my side of the bed.

~

It didn't start out that way, of course. Russ and I met sophomore year at Boston College, through a mutual friend. I thought his Ramones T-shirts and black leather jacket were cool, and I fell for him when he told me he was a member of the Coalition to End Nuclear War (this was the '80s) and had carried a mock nuclear warhead across campus during a protest. We were not that couple who was inseparable, in part because he studied more and I socialized more, and at the time, neither of us entertained a future together. We had an extended group of mutual friends, all of us enjoying the vibrancy of nearby Boston and reveling in BC in its heyday, when quarterback Doug Flutie won the Heisman Trophy and propelled the school into the national spotlight.

Yet almost to our surprise, our relationship deepened beyond the casual college romance; we were married 10 days after Russ graduated from medical school. He was so busy he forgot to get a haircut, and in our wedding pictures, his curly blond hair is blowing in the wind. The day we returned from our honeymoon, we moved into an apartment we found on East 84th Street—our first time living together.

It wasn't easy being married to a medical resident. A month after our wedding, Russ began his training as an ob-gyn in the Bronx. He left our apartment at 6 a.m. and worked until 7 p.m. the following night. When he got home, exhausted, he cuddled next to me on our floral Jennifer Convertible sofa and cried. It wasn't just that he hadn't slept in 36 hours, but that the job was so much more physically and emotionally demanding than he thought it would be, and the burden of responsibility felt enormous. As I comforted him, I thought, *What did I get myself into?* He started another 36-hour shift the next morning.

Back then, medical residents in New York City still worked up to 120 hours a week, which meant that much of the time, I was alone. When he did show up to social events on rare occasions, some friends took to calling him Rent-a-Russ, joking that I found clones of Russ to go out with in his absence.

But there was nothing funny about how quickly our relationship soured. Some nights, he was so exhausted that he could barely hold a conversation. Meanwhile, I was eager to chat and go out with friends as we always had. I was temping at a midtown office and writing for a local newspaper, which meant I had much more time on my hands than he did. The real problem was that I needed more of his attention and time, and he had none to give.

By the end of the first year, I was already a bit worried about whether our marriage would last. While the divorce rate among doctors is lower than the national average, there is evidence that when they are still medical residents, they are *more* likely to divorce. A study conducted two years after we were married, in 1992, found that the divorce rate among doctors in certain medical specialties climbed to more than 50% compared with 20% in others. One of Russ's classmates from medical school, a surgery resident, had married on Labor Day and was already separated by Christmas.

But things began looking up when I enrolled in journalism school, because the nine-month master's program kept me engaged and busy. Then I took a job at a health magazine after graduation, which I loved, while his schedule—and stress level—eased a bit.

As time went on, we came to resemble other hard-working young professionals. We fell into a groove, and didn't dwell on starting a family. Once I did get pregnant, Russ was endlessly attentive and happy to answer my millions of questions. But after Michael was born—not so much. Worse, when Michael was only a few months old and still nursing through the night, Russ decided to train for the New York City marathon, which meant that when he got home, instead of taking the baby from my arms, he would give us a quick kiss and go out for incrementally longer runs, up to 15 miles. Now, I was the one who was tired and stressed.

It's not that Russ didn't help with the baby. He took a shift with Michael almost every night, cradling and rocking our son in a special dance they both seemed to love. But come bedtime, he'd pop in earplugs so he could sleep while I woke every two hours to feed Michael. He did the same when Katie was born two years later, with the (legitimate) excuse that he had to be alert for his job, but I resented it. To me, it seemed as if the kids and I weren't a priority.

Long before I met my future husband, my mother used to caution, "Never marry a doctor; you'll always come last." I thought of those words many times over the years as I stockpiled resentments, a telltale sign, according to relationship experts, that the marriage would not last. I still stew over the time Russ scheduled himself to work a 24-hour shift in the hospital on my birthday, which fell on a Saturday. While the kids played out back, the doorbell rang, and I opened it to find a delivery guy holding a dozen long-stem roses. I smiled, then read the card. The flowers were from the best man at our wedding and his wife, both physicians, who were sympathetic when they heard I would be alone that day.

Sometimes I'd complain to Russ's face, but mostly I seethed; I became an expert in grudge-holding and did little to change the dynamic of the relationship, eventually becoming accustomed to what I considered my husband's benign neglect.

Still, on a day-to-day basis, it felt as if there was intimacy and friendship between us, and I thought of us as a good match. I've always loved that in contrast to my worrying nature, Russ is exuberantly glass-half-full. He is literally the fisherman who casts his rod week after week and believes that this time he will reel in the Big One.

I am not speaking metaphorically. Besides running, he had bought himself a small boat to pursue his passion for fishing—an activity he mostly did without us. Sometimes after one of those sojourns on the water, I'd give him the silent treatment, until eventually, one or the other of us would make an overture and we'd reconcile. In my heart, I was still over the moon for my husband who was so smart and still freaking adorable. Besides, a little makeup sex went a long way.

Until the next time.

I knew there were plenty of couples who worked long hours, so why did my situation feel so different? I think it was because his work as an ob-gyn who brings new life into the world, racing through traffic to deliver a baby, seemed to trump what I did—taking care of the kids and writing low-paying articles—making me feel less-than. During those early years of parenthood, I felt like a light bulb left on around the clock, illuminating the rest of my family. When their lights flickered, I shone brighter, worked harder. As a result, I felt myself fading, burning out, and eclipsed.

Russ often encouraged me to take time for myself, but I was so frazzled by parenting young children, working, and doing daily chores that I didn't even try to find hobbies. Just the thought of leaving my kids with a babysitter to do something other than work left me guilt-ridden. I can't imagine I was any different from other new mothers. I believed in the mantra "The days are long, but the years are short." I fervently hoped this stage would pass and reminded myself that it *was* a stage. There were many aspects of my life I was grateful for—health, kids, family, friends—and I was aware that I led a privileged life. But it wasn't the life or marriage I had envisioned. What I couldn't accept was the feeling that Russ didn't automatically step up when I needed him.

Fortunately for our family, I was raised Catholic, which meant divorce was a last resort, something that was never seriously on the table. I was just anxious and tired. *This, too, shall pass*, I thought. Then Michael was diagnosed with Tourette.

~

On top of everything, a week after Michael's ticcing began, I started a new job teaching an introductory journalism class at Quinnipiac University, an hour or so from our home. Over the years, I had been working less and less and feeling more and more isolated. I yearned to do something more fulfilling than volunteering for the Girl Scouts and the cultural enrichment committee at our local elementary school. But I was worried I couldn't live up to my admittedly fraught definition of a good mom *and* work full-time, given the demands of Russ's practice and my own disorganized tendencies. So I made do with pitching in part-time as a receptionist at Russ's office as well as planning his lectures, helping to market his practice, and writing articles for his website and newsletter. But the setup wasn't ideal—too much togetherness!—and I felt as if my talents and education were going to waste.

When the opportunity to work in academia arose, I jumped. I figured the gig would be the perfect fit for me, that I could zip up and back to campus while the kids were in school. I had loved studying journalism and working as a journalist, and the idea of teaching college students about First Amendment freedoms, ethics, and objectivity was energizing. Plus, I had to teach in person for only two-and-a-half hours a week. *How hard could it be?*

Answer: very. And the timing couldn't have been worse.

On my first day—and my first day ever as a teacher—I stood behind the podium with 25 students staring up at me and realized I had no idea what to do. For the past 10 days, I had been at home with Michael, thinking only about his tics. I had barely showered, never mind prepared for this moment. Fortunately, the department chair had sent me a syllabus used by the last professor, so I relied on that document, took attendance, and gave students a brief bio: After journalism school, I had worked in New York City for a health magazine owned by *Reader's Digest,* and then moved to D.C. and freelanced for several years, also for health, parenting, and women's magazines. I had also written a book about the Red Cross.

Fifteen minutes into the 75-minute class, I'd run out of things to say. I was also distracted. After all of my research into Tourette, it was Russ who had ended up taking Michael to see the neurologist—since the earliest appointment we could get coincided with my first day in class. (Bad form if I missed my first day). Aside from pediatrician appointments when Michael was an infant (since the doctor's office happened to be in the same building as Russ's office), my husband rarely came with me when either child had a doctor's visit. I was grateful he was taking a morning off from work to bring Michael in, but I was also afraid of missing something important.

When my phone rang and I saw it was my husband, I excused myself to take the call. (Also bad form.) *I can't do anything right,* I thought as I stepped outside the classroom. *Bad mother. Bad teacher. Lord, help me.*

Before I left home that morning, I had handed Russ the black composition notebook I had begun using to list and organize all my research and resources. Inside, I had taped the doctor's address and numbers as well as his credentials—medical school, residencies, fellowships, and board certifications. They were impressive. I'd also taped a typewritten list of questions into my notebook for Russ to ask:

> *How long do you think he'll continue to miss school?*
>
> *What drugs should he be on?*
>
> *Can he function in the public school system?*
>
> *Are there any treatments that might work? Ask about the side effects of meds.*
>
> *Get a diagnosis! Is it Tourette?*

During my years as a health journalist, I'd interviewed many prominent physicians, from Dr. Ruth to the surgeon general, and I approached this appointment in a similarly methodical manner.

Truthfully, I had my reservations about the neurologist, the same doctor we'd taken Michael to when he was 7 or so and had first started ticcing. Like all the other doctors we'd talked to, he'd reassured me that our son would likely outgrow the tics. Now we were back.

As I stood there holding my cellphone, waiting for answers from my husband, I allowed myself to feel a moment of hope. But when Russ spoke, he didn't have any answers. Instead, he told me that after spending a few minutes with Michael, the neurologist had said, "This is striking."

"No kidding," I said. "What else?"

"He gave us a note to give to the school."

"What does it say?"

"Michael will be out of school for two weeks or more due to a neurologic problem."

"Is there a diagnosis?"

He paused. "He said that Michael has Tourette."

We had already figured that out, but hearing the words seemed life-changing.

"He gave us a prescription for a drug called Tenex." I had read about Tenex and knew it was an anti-hypertensive drug originally prescribed to treat high blood pressure, but that it was sometimes also used to treat kids with attention deficit hyperactivity disorder (ADHD) and tic disorders. Though I'd read that it didn't always work for kids with Tourette, and that it could cause drowsiness, I was reassured that Michael would be taking a medication prescribed to tens of thousands of kids across the country.

According to Russ, when the doctor handed over the prescription, he said, "Maybe you'll get lucky."

"Maybe we'll get lucky?!" I repeated. "That's it?"

"He told us to call Yale."

It was a huge letdown. I was hoping for more. I was hoping for answers.

"I already did."

I had already discovered that when it comes to Tourette, there were a handful of medical centers around the country that offered specialized care, including the Yale Child Study Center—an hour from our home. Yale is now one of 21 Centers of Excellence, a program launched by the TAA in 2014 to identify medical institutions that provide a high level of coordinated clinical care and conduct research.

I was waiting for a packet from Yale that we needed to fill out and send back before we could make an appointment. Michael had missed more than a week of classes already. More waiting.

I ended class early, using the excuse that it was our first session, then I stopped at Dunkin' Donuts. During the drive home, I drank coffee and ate a Boston creme donut while I planned my next move.

That night, I grilled Russ for more details.

"What was the doctor like? Did he seem to know a lot about Tourette?" I asked.

"He's the kind of guy who probably sees some patients with a lot of big problems, but he sees some with little problems. He probably doesn't see someone like Michael—a kid ticcing nonstop—very often." Russ paused, then added what for him was an admission of disappointment. "I thought he was going to be the guy with all of the answers. He's the go-to pediatric neurologist in the area, but it's clear he doesn't see this very often, and it's clearly something he refers to another specialist." Russ paused again.

"I guess it was kind of a letdown. I was surprised when he started telling me about Yale. I figured he would be more familiar with cases like Michael's. It struck me that Michael must have a severe case."

"Did Michael tic while you were there?" I pressed.

"Oh, yeah," he said. "I walked out of the office a little surprised and stunned."

As Russ spoke, I emptied the dishwasher. I thought he was finished, because he went quiet, but then he continued. It took him forever, but he finally got to what was really on his mind. I wasn't sure why he was stalling.

"That's when Michael and I walked to the lab area of the hospital to get his bloodwork done. Michael started ticcing when we walked in...."

As Russ made small talk with the nurse, who was Black, our son said the N-word. The nurse ignored him. Then he said it again.

Why do people with coprolalia, derived from the Greek word *kopra* which means "feces" and *lalia* which means "speech" (literally, "shit-talk") say taboo words and use racial and ethnic slurs? Others make obscene gestures, known as copropraxia. Together, the two are known as coprophenomena, and why they occur is one of the most confounding aspects of Tourette.

The information I'd read on the TAA's website wasn't exactly enlightening. "Like other tics, the root of this symptom is physical—that is, there is a neurobiological basis to coprolalia and copropraxia. Fortunately, only a minority of individuals with Tourette syndrome experience coprophenomena. However, for those with coprolalia who are trying to deal with the world—in public places, school, at home or work—just getting through the day can be excruciatingly difficult."

It is true that cursing can occur after other brain injuries, as British neurologist Oliver Sacks chronicled in several of his best-selling books. Coprolalia has also been associated with abnormalities in the brain's neurotransmitters, including dopamine and serotonin, which help regulate impulse control, pleasure, and mood. The most recent theories, based on brain imaging, implicate the basal ganglia and thalamus, which are involved primarily in motor control.

Years later, the most satisfying, straightforward answer I came across was from Dr. John Walkup, a Tourette syndrome expert and chair of the Pritzker Department of Psychiatry and Behavioral Health at the Ann and Robert H. Lurie Children's Hospital of Chicago. He explained that kids with tic disorders have a very thin "stimulus barrier," meaning that if they have post-nasal drip, they'll cough or sniff because there's a little irritation back there; if they wear a turtleneck or a tight shirt, they will have neck tics; if they see a Black person, they'll think of epithets; if they see an attractive person, they might use an inappropriate word.

In other words, it's not unusual for someone with coprolalia to see a person of color, then use a racial epithet in the presence of that person. As Dr. Walkup explained, "Their stimulus barrier is so thin that all that stuff deep in the primitive part of the brain breaks through," he said. "So there's a stimulus, it triggers a racial response, and out it comes. And it's the same thing with sexual matters."

Whatever the cause, even the Tourette community has a difficult time reconciling coprolalia. In 2021, the TAA ran an awareness campaign called "Dropping F(act)-Bombs."

"We received a lot of angry feedback," recalled Amanda Talty, president and CEO of the TAA. On the one hand, she heard complaints from people who had Tourette but did not have coprolalia—most of those with Tourette don't—who accused the TAA of perpetuating the stigma around Tourette. "On the other hand, people with coprolalia were saying, 'Oh, finally, a nod to us,'" she told me.

Since then, Talty said the organization has been careful not to use language "minimizing or othering" members of the Tourette community who have coprolalia. Rare though it is, coprolalia is "one of, if not the top symptom that prevents people with Tourette from reentering society in the same way other people do," she said. It was the main reason I was keeping Michael home from school, after all.

Of course, Russ did not know any of this when he was at the hospital with Michael. And even though he explained to the nurse in the lab that Michael had Tourette, the incident was upsetting and embarrassing.

"Oh, honey, don't say that," the nurse said to Michael, when he repeated the slur again...and again.

Russ looked over at me. "I felt a little scared because I was thinking, *Is this going to be able to be treated? Is he going to get better? Is he going to have this for the rest of his life?*"

"Welcome to my world," I said.

After witnessing his son call a Black nurse the N-word, my husband was finally unnerved.

Chapter 5

My Defiant Child

Despite some colic, Michael was a cheerful, affectionate, and alert baby, meeting or exceeding all the milestones, including turning over at 3 months, which was not a feat I welcomed. Every night, I would go into his bedroom multiple times to turn him onto his back because I was afraid he would die of SIDS. By 6 months, he was crawling, which meant erecting baby gates on all four levels of our circa-1800s townhouse, with infant-unfriendly hardwood floors. And don't get me started on my freak-outs when we later moved to Connecticut, where the house came with a pool. The reality was, I saw trouble around every corner.

A week or so after Michael was born, I went for a walk around the block—my first alone with my newborn. We lived on a quiet street in the Georgetown neighborhood of D.C., and by the time I made the third turn, I was so exhausted that I almost didn't notice a petite, frail-looking woman with short, silver hair walking right toward me.

"May I?" she asked as she came closer to the stroller.

A bit startled, I said, "Sure."

She peered at my baby as if she were a child staring at a newborn puppy, then said, wistfully, "I love looking at newborn babies because they're so innocent. Before the world has a chance to corrupt them."

With that, she disappeared down the block like an apparition, but her words stayed with me. She'd hit on something. As I saw it, my job as a mother was to make sure the world didn't corrupt my children.

We moved to Connecticut the day after Michael's first birthday, and Katie was born a year later. Any maternal instinct I had developed with Michael was silenced by my daughter's constant crying, which stopped only when I picked her up and held her. She would also sleep in the car, and on nights when Russ was working, I'd drive up and down I-95 until both kids were asleep, ever hopeful. But as soon as I pulled into the driveway, Katie began wailing again. Thus began our nocturnal ritual.

Michael's first complete sentence was, "Mommy, put that baby down." I only wished I could. Then, at 6 months, she magically turned a corner. Instead of wailing, she would make a high-pitched chirping sound, which earned her the nickname "Birdie." From then on, she morphed into a relatively easy infant, then child, at home and school.

Michael, on the other hand, took up more and more of my energy, up at 6 a.m. every morning and ready to go. Like his favorite toy, Thomas the Tank Engine, his motor was always running.

Enrolling him in a tumbling and gymnastics class when he was 2 years old helped; he could do somersaults, jump, and run in a padded, safe space. But things didn't go as well when, a few months later, I signed him up for a Mommy and Me music class called Music Together. I thought he'd be a natural, given how he responded to music early on. When I was pregnant with him, there was a trendy idea, which was later debunked, that listening to classical music would make your baby smarter, even while the baby was in utero, and like every mom-to-be, I received a Baby Mozart DVD at my shower. Watching the video, which featured colorful trains, mobiles, lights, and puppets, with Mozart playing in the background, became baby Michael's favorite activity—a blessing for me.

The music class started well, with Michael sitting and playing the maracas and bongo drums like all the other preschoolers. But inevitably, he would tire of the activity, jumping up and running from corner to corner counterclockwise around the room, like an animal trapped in a cage.

My mother-in-law repeatedly reminded me that the reason she'd had only two children was that my husband was so "bad." I had to correct her on the low-key a few times when she used that word in front of Michael—a real no-no, according to the stack of parenting books piling up on my nightstand. I'd heard the story often about the time she arrived at Russ's elementary school to find her towheaded son running laps around the school building. Russ was so rambunctious that the teacher had sent him outside to let off some steam.

People routinely gave me unsolicited advice about reining Michael in, because that's really what an anxious, sleep-deprived new mother needs—a bunch of strangers telling her how to be a parent. Worse yet was the advice from well-meaning relatives. My mother, who had a Michael of her own, my younger brother, said that "all Michaels are trouble." My brother had been the class clown, the kid who refused to get out of bed until five minutes before we left for school. He also happened to be my mother's favorite child.

Once, when my extended family was renting a house at the Jersey Shore for a week, 3-year-old Michael went missing. After combing the house, a half-dozen of us ran down to the beach or into the street looking for him, screaming his name. The whole time, he was hiding behind a huge TV, pleased with himself for fooling us all. I, however, was far from pleased. It felt embarrassing at times to have a child who didn't listen to me, who simply tuned me out. Sometimes, he would pounce on Katie when I wasn't looking, and hit her—or me. He even hit the pediatrician once, prompting me to ask about Michael's behavior. She referred me to a local psychologist who, after a couple of visits, reassured me that Michael's behavior was "normal" for his age.

I wasn't so sure. Or maybe I just felt overwhelmed parenting two kids and having little help, aside from a babysitter I hired 10 hours a week so I could do some work. Later that year, I posed the kids in front of the Christmas tree for a holiday card photo. Michael got antsy after take number five or six, and he peed on the Christmas tree.

Yet when his preschool teacher recommended I read a book called *Your Defiant Child: Eight Steps to Better Behavior,* I was insulted; indignant, really. I read the book anyway. It was spot-on in its description of Michael: He ignored commands, deliberately disobeyed adults, and violated the rules we had taught him. In a nutshell, the prescription was to replace negative criticism with positive attention and praise. The author wrote: "Creativity is always an asset in child rearing but it can't hold a candle to consistency." It was a lesson I had yet to learn. Soon, I started doing "special time" with Michael as the author advised, allowing him to direct the play. Katie was still napping, so I tried to give Michael one-on-one attention while she was asleep (I would give Katie special time as well).

Later, I would turn to books like *Jump-Starting Boys, Driven to Distraction,* and many others. My goal was to figure out how to bring out the best in Michael and subdue the devilish side. I hoped these books would serve as a road map that displayed the arrows, markers, and danger signs when we hit bumps. And they did help. Between my newfound parenting skills and his natural maturation, Michael's behavior got a little better—until he went to elementary school.

In late September, a month into first grade, I received my first email from Michael's teacher. Soon, I was getting regular notes about how Michael talked out of turn, made mischief with his buddies, or acted impulsively. Michael was fidgety, whistled occasionally, and had trouble focusing on his work. Besides having a Ph.D., she was a veteran teacher who wasn't going to let some punk 6-year-olds get in the way of teaching. She created a reward system with a sticker chart. When Michael earned 10 stickers, he was rewarded with a visit to the prize basket, chock-full of dime-store trinkets.

The approach worked—to an extent. But then his music teacher began emailing me repeatedly. She said that Michael would stand up and growl at children, bang into the chairs next to him, and make "strange noises." "It seemed like he would try anything to get our attention," she said.

Russ and I were surprised he'd acted out in music class, given his affinity for music. We'd discovered that Michael could sing when he was about 7 years old. That's when he began a ritual of singing "Happy Birthday" to family members in his "opera man" voice, complete with vibrato. When they still shared a room, both kids would don faux leather jackets and sunglasses and jump on their beds with air guitars blaring and singing along to Elvis Presley's "Burning Love." Not long after, Michael began taking guitar lessons at a local music store, though his interest seemed tepid, at best.

I defended my son to the teacher, like any good Italian mother. I remember thinking, *Wait until Katie—my perfectly behaved, darling little girl—gets there. I'll prove I really am a good mother.* But I also started to question my parenting skills.

At home I would sometimes scream at Michael as a young boy when he didn't listen or hit Katie. I didn't need parenting books to tell me that yelling wasn't an effective form of discipline. Whenever I lost my temper, I felt guilty, especially because much of the time, my son was playful, good-natured, and curious. And he was passionate about animals—always so sweet and gentle with any living creature. He was the kid who spent summers gently catching and releasing butterflies in his cupped hands in the backyard. One summer, we planted two purple butterfly bushes, which attracted all sorts of species, including Monarchs and Eastern Tiger Swallowtails, and Michael wanted to know all of their names and everything about them, to the extent that we started calling him "nature boy." Most boys his age seemed to be playing sports nonstop, but being outdoors and exploring captivated our son in a way no sport or classroom lesson ever could.

His teachers didn't see this side of Michael—at least not very often. By October of his first-grade year, the principal and school psychologist were being copied on emails. Michael was "off task," not responsive to supervision, and disruptive in class. When I re-read these emails all these years later, I still wince. He ended up in the principal's office so often that I started to feel as though my son was a bad seed.

I joined a "parenting think tank group," taking workshops on how to manage children with behavioral challenges. I also hired a child psychologist turned parenting coach. She was based in Minnesota and would email me all sorts of helpful information, and we would chat occasionally.

The good news from the parenting coach was that my children got plenty of sleep, they weren't overscheduled, I never compared them, I spent a lot of time with them, I read to them incessantly and encouraged reading, and our family had structure—aside from the fact that Dad disappeared sometimes. Since they knew he was off "bringing new life into the world," as we joked, it was all good.

I learned simple language about how to improve a child's behavior, and that praise is one of the most effective motivators for change. For example, instead of telling Michael not to hit his sister, I'd tell the kids to use "kind words and gentle touch." As much as possible, I began to use positive rather than negative discipline tactics and doled out daily rewards for good behavior, like extra cuddle time or story time. And if Michael broke a rule like hitting, I learned to take swift action.

None of this came naturally to me. I took furious notes on the computer, printed them out, and made cheat sheets of effective discipline tactics on sticky notes with cryptic messages like *calm*, *praise*, and *offer alternatives*.

However, the parenting pros also agreed that one thing was clear: I was not firmly in charge. I was wishy-washy in my enforcement of the rules, which creates insecurity, like a dog who bites. "Your word has to be golden," one coach told me.

She also taught me tips for how to teach Katie to protect herself and stay safe, and to set limits and boundaries by stating firmly, "You can't do that to me." While I sometimes felt I wasn't doing enough to protect her, the family joke is that Katie became the strong one, literally, in part because she learned to steel herself against Michael's outbursts.

Consulting parenting experts was very helpful and not very expensive, and it made me feel I had people in my corner. I also felt I had to get the situation under control soon, because one of the mantras that stuck with me was "Little kids, little problems, big kids, big problems."

Chapter 6

What Makes Michael Tick?

When Michael was invited to participate in our local elementary school's "advanced learning program" in second grade, Russ and I told ourselves that maybe he had been getting into trouble because he was bored. But he soon began complaining about the extra work and acting out in class, and it became clear that the program might not be a great fit.

I worried we were putting too much pressure on him. My thinking was, *Let's wait until middle school and high school, when things really count.* Russ disagreed, in part because he said Michael could be tracked into honors classes based on his perceived ability starting from this age, affecting his future in school. Russ wanted Michael to reach his potential. We argued about it for the duration of the school year, and despite Russ's reluctance, we allowed Michael to drop out of the program in third grade (the teacher agreed).

What concerned us was that our son's interest in school continued to decline. The thought that Michael was not living up to what he was capable of struck a nerve with both of us. I had grown up with parents who valued catechism more than calculus, and they sent me to a small Catholic school that was not particularly strong academically. That was one reason Russ and I had moved to our Connecticut town: The local public schools were known for top-notch academics. The flip side of this was that Michael's elementary school had a reputation as a pressure cooker; his classmates were ultra-competitive like their Wall Street parents. A writer interviewed in *The New York Times* who grew up here summed it up best, saying, "There was an undercurrent of competitiveness to everything."

That made it tough for kids who might have special needs—and for their parents. One mother who chaired the school's special needs parent group told me that no one ever came to the meetings. "Everyone's kids are perfect here," she said wryly.

But I wasn't after perfection. All I wanted for Michael—for both our kids—was a happy childhood and good health. My friend's father used to tell her, "There are two things I can give you as a parent that nobody can take away: good teeth and a good education." I was a corny, old-school mom who favored bedtime stories like "The Tortoise and the Hare" to keep the kids grounded and out of the race.

Often, I asked myself, *Why did we move here?* I am not particularly competitive or even goal-oriented. While Russ, like our son, was a hyperactive child, I was relatively lethargic. My most memorable childhood caper occurred when I went missing one day, launching the neighborhood on a hunt, my parents terrified I had fallen into a construction pit near our house. In fact, I was at home, sleeping on the floor behind the couch. Another favorite spot for me to nap was in front of the fridge (an old-fashioned model that emitted hot air), the hum of the motor and the warmth lulling me to sleep. I sometimes joked that my spirit animal was a sloth. And here I was living in the Olympic village of suburban America, among cheetahs.

But Russ and I had moved five times in 10 years, and both of us wanted some permanence. Plus, there were some things about this town that resonated with us. I didn't want to send my kids to a school like the one I had gone to—located in a small farming town, where teachers were often hired based on their sports coaching skills and there were no AP classes to be found.

But where we had landed didn't feel right either. It felt like too much for me and, seemingly, for Michael, who, at age 7, began blinking his eyes repeatedly in the first of what we would later learn were tics. A few months after that, he started grimacing involuntarily. Alarmed, we took him to the pediatric neurologist—the guy who assured us that transient tics were exceedingly common in boys, and that Michael would most likely outgrow them. But by fourth grade, things were no better. Michael's behavioral difficulties continued, and he had an increasingly rough time fitting in.

It didn't help that he made new friends each year, only to be separated from them the following year to prevent troublemakers from being in the same classroom. By then, I felt he might be headed down the wrong path, that he risked becoming what my mom used to call a "juvenile delinquent."

In some ways, Michael had always been a bit of an enigma. For years, Russ and I had been racking our brains, trying to figure out what made him tick, no pun intended. The time-outs and declining grades, all while being incredibly curious and able to focus intensely on engaging activities outside of school—we just couldn't put our fingers on it. Too often, I fell back on reminding (read: blaming) Russ that Michael seemed to be a lot like he had been as a child—a boisterous boy who had to run around the school because he had so much energy.

To try to get to the heart of the mystery, the year before Michael's Tourette diagnosis, we'd brought him in for a full neuro-psych evaluation. To us, it seemed there was a missing piece to the puzzle. Plus, I knew that kids with learning disabilities sometimes went undiagnosed for years, and I didn't want that to happen to our son. Over a six-week period, they tested everything from his IQ to his memory, mood, and personality style, as well as how he processed information. The only significant finding was mild anxiety.

At the time, I didn't know that delays in diagnosis and missed diagnoses are common in people with Tourette. According to a TAA's impact survey in 2018, many families reported that it took up to two years to get a diagnosis. And the CDC has estimated that only half of the children with Tourette end up with a formal diagnosis. Given that, it's not uncommon for adults to learn that symptoms that started in their youth were, in fact, Tourette.

Helene Walisever, a clinical psychologist with Tourette syndrome herself and now a member of the TAA's educational advisory board, recalled going to a dozen different doctors before she was diagnosed with Tourette at age 10, in the late 1970s. Before that, doctors diagnosed a seizure disorder and gave her anti-seizure medication, then sent her to therapy for her "nervous tics." "I had the blinking, head shaking, eyebrow raising, and neck twitching," she said. "But when I started making noises—including throat clearing and barking—my mom ramped up the search for the right doctor," she says, and she finally got the correct diagnosis from a neurologist at New York University.

Tourette is widely considered to be both misdiagnosed and underreported in part because tics can go unrecognized. The number of people with a tic disorder who receive treatment is also quite small because most people aren't impaired by their tics—they're impaired by their comorbidities, explained Dr. Walkup. The fact that most people aren't impaired by their tics also tends to delay diagnosis and treatment. "When they go to a doctor, the doctor just treats their ADHD or their anxiety or OCD," said Dr. Walkup. "They may not even notice a tic." Of course, this wasn't widely known back in 2011.

The fact that tics often start off as fairly innocuous eye blinking or sniffing—movements and sounds that everybody makes—also contributes to delays in diagnosis. "But if a child suddenly starts barking uncontrollably, that's going to get medical attention really quickly," Dr. Coffman said.

I had listened to all the experts who assured me that Michael would outgrow his tics and behavioral issues, and now I blamed myself for that. But now, when I broached the topic of medication for ADHD—prescriptions like Adderall and Ritalin—to counteract Michael's hyperactivity and impulsivity, our pediatrician took them off the table, saying they could exacerbate tics.

The good news for kids with Tourette today is that doctors, psychologists, and other medical professionals are more likely to recognize symptoms of Tourette than they were when my son started ticcing, in part because the TAA and its Centers of Excellence are educating health care professionals. Greater media exposure may also play a role.

"More individuals have become aware that there is such a thing as Tourette syndrome, and when they talk to their pediatrician, it can be confirmed," said Dr. Leckman.

That said, even now, it's still hard to get a handle on the number of Americans with Tourette. The first line on the CDC's page on data and statistics on Tourette states, "We do not know exactly how many children have Tourette syndrome (TS)."

Here's why: The CDC monitors the prevalence of diagnosed Tourette syndrome among U.S. children using what's known as the National Survey of Children's Health. Essentially, it's a poll, asking parents if their child has ever been diagnosed with or currently has Tourette syndrome. These annual surveys are what produced the 0.3 percent figure of American children 6 to 17 years old who had ever been diagnosed with Tourette and the 0.2 percent currently diagnosed with Tourette, a statistic that has remained more or less the same since 2007.

All told, this amounts to roughly 174,000 children in 2019, the last survey from which data is available as of this writing. The problem is, to be included in these tallies, a child must have a diagnosis of Tourette, which, as we discovered with Michael, is difficult to get, despite the fact that the condition is more recognized. That's because the diagnosis requires some specific symptoms, for specific lengths of time: To be diagnosed with Tourette, children must have both motor and verbal tics for at least a year before age 18, and the tics cannot be due to medications or other medical conditions.

One 2020 study summed up the conundrum this way: "The prevalence of Tourette syndrome is difficult to determine because of a variety of factors, including stringent diagnostic criteria, varied assessment methodologies, the need for patients or caregivers to acknowledge the existence of tics, and the need for access to health care."

Another issue is that the criteria used for measuring Tourette can often seem like a moving target. "Epidemiologists would call people and say, "Does anybody in your family have motor or vocal tics, or does anybody in your family have Tourette syndrome?' The answers would be *No, no, no, no,*" said Dr. Coffman, director of the movement disorder program at Children's Mercy Kansas City in Kansas City, MO. "Then they changed the questions to, 'Does anybody in your family have movements or sounds they can't control? If so, what do those sound like? What do those look like?' So, they started to ask about the symptoms as opposed to the diagnoses."

That's when the numbers jumped. So much so that it's no longer considered rare—but more on that later.

~

When Michael was in third grade, we requested a meeting to explore getting him an Individualized Education Program (IEP), which was denied because his grades were slightly above average. I was surprised our request was so easily dismissed. To me, it seemed ass-backward that to access help, your child had to fail first. Instead, Michael was referred to a children's social group called Lunch Bunch, which met once a week in the school psychologist's office. Instead of eating in the cafeteria and goofing off with his friends at recess, he sat in a circle talking about his feelings, not the best solution for a boy who needed to run around and let off steam.

As a journalist, I was anxious to have other medical experts weigh in—but instead of zeroing in on the "right" experts, I played the field like someone who keeps swiping right on Tinder but can't find true love. In addition to the pediatric neurologist, there was the occupational therapist who made Michael dangle from the ceiling using what's known as a sensory swing for $250 an hour, and the prominent child psychiatrist who declared my son "a charming, normal child."

"Should I be concerned about the eye blinking?" I asked.

He said it was common.

"ADHD?"

He shook his head, then paused.

"*You* may have ADD," he told me. "But your son doesn't."

This stung, adding to the guilt I already felt that I wasn't quite up to snuff as a mother. He suggested I meet with the social worker in his office, who could help me get a handle on *my* issues. He didn't specify which issues he was referring to, but I was mortified. (Later, I went home and took an online test to see if I fit the profile; I did not.)

When I think about what we have been through since that day, I find it both comical and frustrating. If just one of the "experts" I consulted had sent us to a Tourette specialist like those at the Yale Child Study Center, where we ended up years later, perhaps Michael's case wouldn't have progressed to a raging case of Tourette. Or maybe it still would have. Hindsight is 20/20, of course, but I still believe it would have made a difference if he had been evaluated, diagnosed, and treated earlier, before his symptoms became so severe.

Instead, as Michael's motor tics came and went, we mostly tried to ignore them. Then, when he was in fourth grade, they became more frequent and noticeable, bringing us back to the neurologist. After an evaluation by his nurse practitioner, we got the same spiel: As long as there were no vocal tics, a telltale sign of Tourette, there was nothing to worry about.

We didn't hear those until a month or so before he began blurting out obscenities. I started to notice Michael making muffled sounds under his breath. At the time, I had other things on my mind—choosing paint colors, buying Christmas gifts, and baking cookies. *How could I have not acted on this?* Still, to my mind, vocal tics meant cursing, or at least saying entire, intelligible words. Michael was merely mumbling. I would later learn that coughing, throat clearing, and sniffing—something Michael had been doing for a couple of years—were also considered "phonic," or a form of simple vocal tics.

I wish I could have been the confident mother who trusted her instincts back then, the mother that Michael needed. I knew in my bones that something wasn't right, but instead, I listened to the doctors, nodding and feeling like a fool and ignoring my instincts as a parent. That is, until my son started rapid-fire cursing.

But as devastated as I was when Michael was finally diagnosed with Tourette, I was also a smidge relieved. At least now, we had an explanation for his behavior, a clue to the mystery.

Chapter 7

The Road to Oz

My nightly Google searches soon led me to a community of folks determined to find alternative therapies to control the symptoms of Tourette. I learned there were two camps of Touretters: folks who believed that tics should be treated without drugs and those who thought prescription medications could help, even though most were not FDA-approved to treat the condition. Even all these years later, there are only three medications explicitly approved by the FDA for the suppression of Tourette-related tics: haloperidol (Haldol), pimozide (Orap), and aripiprazole (Abilify). Yet these medications, which are in a class of drugs known as antipsychotics—were originally developed to treat conditions such as bipolar disorder, not Tourette. And doctors often use other drugs, sometimes in tandem.

"There's not a single medication on the market that was ever designed for or brought to market to treat Tourette," said Dr. Coffman.

As for me, I was open to natural approaches. I thought back to when I was nursing Michael and a lactation consultant put me on fenugreek, a funky-tasting herb I swallowed in capsule form several times a day. It was supposed to boost milk production, and it worked. I suspected that Russ might be open to alternative treatments as well. His medical practice blended mainstream approaches with some complementary and alternative medicine (known as CAM), and he had become quite knowledgeable in the area, which I found reassuring.

Nevertheless, I decided our first line of attack should be a mainstream medicine approach, though I'd keep the natural approaches on the back burner, in case Michael didn't show improvement soon.

Soon was the operative word. After six days of keeping Michael home from school and listening to him curse a blue streak, I was at my wit's end. He was afraid to leave the house because he didn't want anyone to hear him tic. I had the same fear, plus I worried that my son was restless and unpredictable. As a result, I rarely left the house except to do essential errands. When I did make a run to the grocery store, I inevitably came home with a jumbo chocolate bar for myself, which I kept hidden in my purse. It was my little reward, my emergency chocolate, and I didn't intend to share it.

One night after dinner, Russ and I sat down at the kitchen island to begin filling out the 80 pages of paperwork required before we could get an appointment at the Yale Child Study Center, including a 26-page questionnaire and separate parent and child intake forms.

In addition to a family medical history, there were six pages of questions about the onset, type, and frequency of Michael's tics: *Do the tics occur in clusters (bouts) during the course of the day? Do the tics typically go through periods when they are worse and then become better again?* Answers to both: yes. *Have the tics varied, with some tics*

53

disappearing and new tics taking their place over time? Are the tics more noticeable during periods of stress or emotional excitement? Yes and yes.

A few days after I'd mailed our forms to Yale, I called to follow up and was thrilled to learn that we were *in*. After two weeks of Michael's ticcing and missing school, we were going to see a bona fide expert, get some answers, and, I hoped, get our lives back to normal.

Or so I thought. It turned out that the next available appointment was in May, more than three months away.

"But it's coprolalia—he's cursing nonstop," I said, my voice trembling, hoping that using the lingo would help get me in the door. "He hasn't been to school in two weeks. It's an emergency."

Not to Yale. Apparently, they were used to coprolalia, and worse. I tried to keep the receptionist on the phone. "But he can't go to *school*. He barely leaves the *house*," I begged. (I was not above begging.) It was no use. Three months it would be. All I could do was mark the date on my calendar and hope the Tenex prescribed by the pediatric neurologist would work in the meantime. *What the hell am I going to do between now and then?*

The answer was to drag Michael to more doctors. He had already seen a pediatrician and a pediatric neurologist. He was about to start weekly talk therapy sessions with a social worker recommended by the school. And I'd also gotten an appointment with a psychiatrist named Dr. Kevin Kalikow in nearby Westchester County, NY, who'd agreed to squeeze us in. Dr. Kalikow was the author of a book titled *Your Child in the Balance*, and he later published a second book titled *Kids on Meds*.

When I filled in Dr. Kalikow beforehand on the phone, I told him that Michael could be moody but was generally happy and good-natured. Despite the tics, "there was no excess sadness or hopelessness," as he put it. And while my son could get frustrated easily, especially recently, he had no history of explosions or excessive anxiety.

When it was time to join Michael in the office, the doctor cut to the chase: "Well, I'm happy about all the things I'm *not* seeing," he smiled. I assumed he was referring to conditions like OCD and ADHD, which, as I'd learned, are also common in kids with Tourette. Dr. Kalikow later told me that Michael showed no signs of depression or chronic anxiety either.

I wasn't at the point where I considered this to be good news; I was still fixated on the near-constant sounds and full-on curse words emanating from my 11-year-old's mouth.

But I could tell the doctor was trying to be reassuring when he turned to Michael and said, "You're burdened by Tourette, but you're likable, not anxious, you get along well with Mom and Dad, and you're smart—you don't have learning problems." Michael asked why he cursed. "That's not clear," Dr. Kalikow said. "It has something to do with the way the brain works—the place that comes up with tics is connected to bad words." I was grateful that the doctor could at least explain things to Michael—or at least be clear about what he didn't have—with an authority I could not.

Dr. Kalikow waited for Michael to respond, and when my son remained silent, he gently asked, "Do you have any more questions?"

Michael was quiet for a minute, then asked, "Why did this happen to me?"

I looked over at him, surprised he was being so open, at least compared with interactions he'd had with other doctors we'd seen. He seemed so small sitting in the big leather wingback chair across from the doctor's imposing mahogany desk, ticcing away. *God, he must be so scared and confused,* I thought.

"You know, I don't know," Dr. Kalikow replied thoughtfully, touching his hand to his head. "It's kind of like asking, "Why am I bald?"

Michael didn't laugh or even smile; he just sat there and thought about it. But I think he was reassured by this analogy. I was, too, because I have never heard a more plainspoken, truthful answer.

Then Michael asked, "Did I do this to myself?" This was my first real clue as to what my son had been thinking about his tics. My first thought: *Is my Catholic guilt hereditary?!* "No, it's part of your biology. You didn't do anything wrong," Dr. Kalikow replied soothingly. "You're not a bad person. Actually, a bunch of kids have tics."

Michael nodded, then asked, a bit hesitantly, "Is Tourette for your whole life?"

"Generally, no." The doctor then explained, as I had before, that a lot of kids outgrow the symptoms of Tourette as they get older.

Though Michael hadn't said anything about feeling ashamed of his condition, Dr. Kalikow must have known this, because as we wrapped up the session, he explained to Michael that there was no reason to keep the Tourette a secret. "Other people need to be educated," he said. He suggested that Michael go back to school and get out of the house.

I wasn't sure that was going to happen. So far, Michael had refused to tell his friends from school about his tics, or talk to them at all. I worried that his embarrassment would become a real obstacle to his recovery and possibly lead to something I had read about called school refusal. That was one reason I had ramped up my efforts to persuade Michael to go back to school—especially now that we had three months to wait before our appointment at Yale.

He had no interest in returning; all he could think about was what other students would think. But Michael also understood that every day he was absent, he became more of a curiosity, which created a conundrum. Still, he was loath to expose himself to hundreds of potentially mocking middle-schoolers, who, he was convinced, were all "perfect," unlike him. Indeed, our longest conversations during this limbo period tended to be about what he'd tell kids about his absence when he finally *did* return.

"What if I said that I had mono?" he suggested one afternoon when we were playing Hangman on the red couch.

"But you're usually not out of school for that long with mono."

"Or I could say I broke my leg and I needed surgery."

"You don't have a cast."

"Can I get one? Or one of those boots?"

"Why don't you tell the kids the truth like Dr. Kalikow suggested?" I asked. "Maybe you can help educate kids. The Tourette Association even has something called the Youth Ambassador program where they will bring a volunteer—a kid with Tourette syndrome—to talk to your class and educate your classmates and teachers about Tourette."

I'd read about this program early on, where kids from ages 12 to 17 with Tourette and tic disorders would speak to their peers at school (or on sports teams or in scouting troops) to convey the facts about Tourette and promote tolerance and understanding. I was all jazzed up about it and even imagined Michael applying to become a Youth Ambassador one day. I envisioned him learning to advocate for himself, doing local media interviews and meeting with elected officials. As usual, I had high hopes.

Helene Walisever also told me about a buddy program run by the local TAA chapter that paired older kids with Tourette with younger ones. Unfortunately, Michael showed no interest in mingling with other children with Tourette, including attending the summer camp I'd found called "Twitch and Shout," for kids with tics.

Desperate for anything to tide us over, I called the number Dr. Kalikow had handed me—for a scientist who was researching CBIT (comprehensive behavioral intervention for tics). To my surprise, Denis Sukhodolsky Ph.D., picked up his own phone.

CBIT is different from CBT (cognitive behavioral therapy), a type of talk therapy that helps people identify and change destructive thought patterns and behaviors. In contrast, CBIT is what's known as *habit reversal therapy,* which aims to rid people of unwanted behaviors or habits. CBIT was developed specifically for people with tics, teaching them to become more aware of their *premonitory urges,* a sensation or feeling that needs to be satisfied immediately and occurs in more than 80% of people with Tourette, including Michael. The tic relieves that urgency, similar to scratching an itch, but more extreme. (Years later, Michael described it as "the worst itch of your life. If you don't scratch it, you will go crazy.")

CBIT teaches people how to react with a competing behavior or response when they experience a premonitory urge. For instance, when someone feels a tic coming on, they might respond with deep breathing instead of swearing.

As I gave the doctor my spiel, telling him how Michael cursed constantly, wouldn't go outside, and refused to go to school, I felt both hopeful and desperate.

Dr. Sukhodolsky said he would like to evaluate Michael to see if he was a candidate for the study, but that he had to meet with a Yale physician first. He told us he would need to arrange an appointment with Dr. Robert King, medical director of the Yale Child Study Center's Tic and Obsessive-Compulsive Disorder Program. Suddenly, we were bumped to the head of the line—with an appointment to get in at the end of the week!

Woot! Woot! We were going to Yale!

Excited, I called Russ and asked him to clear his schedule so he could come to the appointment. "I have patients all morning on that day," he said.

I was seething. But I didn't yell. Or cry. Instead, I said, "If President Obama's daughter had the symptoms our son has, he'd go with his wife to the appointment, and no one has a busier schedule than him. You are a doctor, this is a top specialist, and I need you there." For good measure, I explained how helpful it was for a layperson (me) to show up at a doctor's appointment with an actual doctor (him). In return, I got a lecture about how much money he would lose if he canceled patients for an entire morning.

I resented what I saw as his rigidity, but on some level, I also got it. As a male ob-gyn in a world where many women patients prefer women doctors, Russ was struggling to stay afloat, working around the clock, and paying nearly $100,000 a year in malpractice insurance (typical for doctors in his field), though he had a spotless record. As a result, he was watching every penny.

I knew this, but I didn't back down. When Russ got home that night, I didn't speak to him. Instead, as we lay silently in bed that night, I rehashed every quarrel we'd ever had, every grudge I'd ever held, like how he continued wearing earplugs at night long after I'd stopped breastfeeding and needed to get up for the kids. Or the fact that he couldn't attend most parent-teacher conferences because of work, yet somehow managed to arrange his schedule around the tides, taking off afternoons in summer on a weekly basis to go fishing. My mother had been right about doctors: I felt as if I always came last. But the kids too? *Our* kids? I was so angry I felt like kicking him as he lay watching the news.

The truth is, I didn't expect Russ to be doting. I knew he loved me and that he had confidence in my abilities as a person and a parent, but I didn't feel confident in myself. This was the hardest thing I had ever done, ever faced, and I felt as if I were crumbling.

Fuming, I got up from our bed and went to sleep in the spare bedroom. This would become a habit—one that made me feel even more isolated than I already was, stuck in the house with a cursing 11-year-old. Looking back, I had a tendency to focus on Russ's flaws and forget his sweetness, like the way he tirelessly bodysurfed with our son when we were at the Jersey Shore, or how he taught both kids to fish and ski, or how he took them on long hikes at the local Audubon Center and taught them to identify birds, bugs, and plants. But I felt blindsided, first by Michael's Tourette and then by Russ's seeming refusal to put Michael first. And so, my resentment, which had been building for a decade, took on new layers, like ice forming on top of a glacier.

A speaker at one of the many lectures and meetings I attended had mentioned that the divorce rate among parents of kids with learning disabilities was well over 50 percent. When I got home, I looked it up and discovered that was an exaggeration, but there was evidence that the stress of parenting a child with any sort of disability did put a strain on a marriage, and I worried that Tourette would break us. I knew my paltry salary as an adjunct professor and freelance journalist couldn't feed me or the kids, let alone pay the mortgage, which made me feel terrible about myself on top of everything. Plus, I still loved Russ. And I actually liked him too—most of the time.

A few papers cite a higher divorce rate among parents of kids with ADHD, while some research indicates that the experience brings parents closer together. Not so much for us.

The next night, Russ surprised me. "I canceled my patients for the morning. I can come to the appointment." I was so relieved, and grateful. That night, I grabbed my pillow and moved back into our bed. We did not discuss what changed his mind, but Russ later told me, "My whole thinking was warped because all I thought about was making money. I didn't want to go bankrupt."

On February 2, Michael, Russ, and I drove a good hour and a half to New Haven, through a slippery mix of snow and sleet. In a way, I felt like Dorothy approaching Oz. My world had been turned upside down by a twister, but after some false starts along the way, we were about to meet the wizard. In fact, I still have the printout of directions to Yale from Mapquest, slipped inside my trusty notebook, now faded pink from the snow that day, like melted cotton candy.

~

Dr. King reminded me of Einstein, with wiry gray hair that fanned out over his bald spot. His office was a maelstrom of papers and books piled inside and alongside bookshelves. But I forgot about that as he began asking Michael questions about his life, listening intently as my son whistled, squeaked, and mumbled curse words every few seconds between answers. Dr. King later wrote in his report that throughout the interview, Michael's tics were observed at a frequency of every three seconds.

As we sat there, it seemed like a meet-and-greet session, and we chatted about all sorts of topics in addition to Michael's medical history.

"What are your hobbies?"

"How do you do in school?"

"Do you have friends?"

Michael told him that he didn't have a best friend, or a group of kids he spent time with.

The doctor made a note as Michael said that he liked to ski, and to fish with his dad on the Long Island Sound.

"Anything else?"

"I sing in the school choir."

When asked what he wanted to be when he grew up, Michael replied, "I want to live in Vermont in a home with a big yard and farm animals." His answer was so serious and specific that everyone chuckled, which helped break the tension in the room.

I wasn't sure where Dr. King was going with this line of questioning, but I remember thinking that despite his Tourette and his behavioral challenges at school, Michael probably seemed like a pretty typical 11-year-old.

After the discussion, during which Michael had also mentioned that he felt better when things were in their proper place, Dr. King told us that Michael had "a touch" of OCD and a "moderately severe" case of Tourette, which made me wonder what severe looked like.

Dr. King explained that, typically, Tourette symptoms were most severe between ages 11 and 13. He also told us that tics could get worse following periods of stress and mentioned Michael's switch from elementary to middle school as well as our house renovation as possible triggers. "In many cases, the tics will improve or subside spontaneously in the early high school years," he said reassuringly.

He also suggested a medication I'd read about, called Risperdal. I knew from my research that the drug was in a class of second-generation antipsychotic medicines shown to be effective in treating kids with tics, like Abilify. But giving Michael an "antipsychotic" used to treat disorders like schizophrenia seemed like too much too soon.

Russ agreed with me, and as I listened to him chat with the doctor about medications, I was glad he was there. But when Russ said that the two of us wanted to wait to see if the Tenex worked, Dr. King reminded us that it might take weeks to see any effects.

Meanwhile, he also recommended that Michael see Dr. Sukhodolsky, who could teach him CBIT, explaining that recent research indicated that it reduced tics in kids with Tourette. He also emphasized, as Dr. Kalikow had, that it was important that Michael get back to school as soon as possible because he needed to interact with his peers.

Finally, Dr. King suggested that we continue to focus on and reinforce Michael's talents and strengths—like music. At the time, that seemed to me like garden-variety parenting advice. It turned out to be anything but.

As his colleague Dr. Leckman, now the Neison Harris Professor of Child Psychiatry, Psychology, and Pediatrics at the Yale School of Medicine, told me recently, "A focal point for me is really trying to identify the strengths and interests of the child and helping families focus on what the kids are good at, what they like to do, and, moving forward, what they would like to do with their lives. Reinforcing their desires is a crucial part of our clinical intervention. Some families are delighted and reassured with that approach. Others just want to talk about the tics and the treatments."

I was in the latter camp, at least back then, and I walked away a bit disappointed. I was willing to have Michael try the CBIT, but I had convinced myself that the experts at Yale would help heal Michael quickly, as unrealistic as that might have been.

Looking back, my impatience and expectations were laughable. There are people who spend a lifetime looking for effective treatments for Tourette, experimenting with different drugs, to no avail. I didn't realize it yet, but our quest had only just begun.

As I reflect on these early experiences, I realize that these experts were trying to tell me, perhaps subtly, to slow down and try to be patient. Later, a friend of ours named Jacques, who was an acupuncturist working in Russ's office, said much the same thing, cautioning me that Michael's symptoms were not going to go away overnight. "The challenge for you," he said, "is to accept Michael for who he is and to help him learn to accept himself."

I was not there yet.

Chapter 8

How to Get to Carnegie Hall

Thump. Thump. *Thump.*

Here he goes again, I thought.

"Michael!" I yelled from the bottom of the stairs. No answer.

I glanced at Russ, who locked eyes with me for a second.

"Michael, you have to finish your homework," I called up half-heartedly, rising from the couch and trudging up the stairs to his room, where I found my son sprawled sideways on his bed with his feet propped against the wall.

Every few seconds his body jerked, and he punched the air. He coughed. He gurgled. He grunted. Then he kicked the wall again.

Thump.

"I hate my life. I'll never be normal."

64

When I reached down to hug him, his body stiffened. "We're going to get through this together. You'll get better. You just started taking the medication. The doctor said it could take 12 weeks to work."

He kicked at me but didn't reach.

"There *is* no cure," he said, parroting what he had learned while watching a few videos. "I'm a freak."

"Michael, don't say that. You're letting it get to you. Remember the saying from the video? 'I have Tourette's, but Tourette's doesn't have me?'"

"But it does have me." He started to cry. "It *does*."

I knew what he meant. It had me too.

One of the therapists I talked to early on told me I needed to keep my feelings to myself and pretend to be stoic. "And if you don't feel stoic, you have to *act* like you are."

Now I was sobbing in front of Michael.

I tried to compose myself, and then I took Michael by the arm and pulled him into the bathroom for what would become a repeat performance.

"Do you see what I see?" I yelled, both of us looking in the mirror. "I see a young, bright, beautiful boy who can do and be anything he wants to be."

These were almost the exact words my father had said to me the day after I graduated from college, and they had stuck with me. I believed, based on my own experience as a child, that unconditional love was the best gift any parent could give. But combing through all of those parenting books had also taught me a few tricks, including how to properly express approval of my kids' achievements: by being specific and by praising their effort, not the outcome. At that moment, I forgot all of those lessons and instead began to ramble.

"Think of all the good things in your life: You have a family who loves you...you're bright and funny and good at playing drums and guitar...and your voice...it's *heaven sent!*"

The world-weary look on my son's face signaled that he didn't believe a word I was saying. Then he broke free of my grasp and escaped back to his bedroom, where he promptly began kicking the wall again.

I later learned that these outbursts were known as rage attacks or, more clinically, intermittent explosive disorder (IED), a sign of emotional overload. IED can occur in roughly half of kids with Tourette.

Unlike a tantrum, where a child acts out because they have a goal in mind—to get what they want—a rage attack is simply an avalanche of anger. Or, in Michael's case, anger mixed with deep sadness. Like a lot of other aspects of Tourette, it's unclear why some kids have rage attacks and others don't, or whether they are even a distinct diagnosis. But the best response, I would learn, was to give the child space rather than try to reason with him. I was doing the opposite.

"I don't have any friends," Michael wailed. "I'll never have friends." *Thump.*

This was partly true. Michael hadn't had a best friend in years. "That's not so," I protested weakly, naming some girls in our neighborhood whom Michael spent time with.

"They're girls," he snapped. "They don't count. Besides, I'll never have a girlfriend. I'll never get married."

"Of course you will!" I shouted, though I was worried about this too.

Next came a statement that always made me wince: "Katie's perfect."

Another tidbit I learned from reading all of those parenting books is to never compare your kids. But on that night, I did it anyway.

"Katie *seems* perfect," I said. "But she's not—she just *acts* perfect at school." The truth was that, on the surface, at least, I did have one child who seemed flawless.

"She doesn't have Tourette. She doesn't have allergies or asthma. She doesn't wear contacts. *She's not fat.*" He spat the words at me.

66

This was another half-truth. Michael was not fat, but he was a bit overweight, and self-conscious about it.

Russ, who was standing in the doorway, walked in and sat on the bed.

"Let me talk to him."

"No," Michael said, tears pooling in his eyes. "Mom is the only one I feel comfortable with."

Though he loved his outings with Russ, since he'd begun ticcing, Michael had latched on to me, and, aside from my two-day-a-week teaching stint, we were as inseparable as a mother and her infant. I worried that without me by his side, he wouldn't be able to function. I also worried that my constant presence was making a bad situation worse.

That night, Russ did end up sitting with Michael. I slipped out of the room to hide in our bathroom, locking the door and lying on the cold, hard tiles, staring up at the ceiling, glassy-eyed and spent. It was overwhelming, and so upsetting to watch our son suffer like this and feel unable to help him.

The next morning, I poured myself a cup of coffee in a to-go cup, along with a mug for Michael's new tutor, Carol, who had just arrived. Once he'd missed three weeks of school for health reasons, state regulations said he was entitled to two hours a day of free tutoring, through a service known as "homebound instruction." Frankly, I was relieved to have another adult on duty, and as I grabbed my purse, a bottle of water, and my canvas book bag for the commute to my still-newish job, Michael and Carol were already sitting on the couch reading *Tom Sawyer*.

It had been only a few weeks since his at-home lessons had started, but Michael already seemed to adore Carol, who, when she wasn't keeping him focused on math, science, and reading, brought him homemade chocolate chip cookies. The two of them often took breaks to chat like old friends, although Michael sometimes called her "bitch" to her face. But as they sat on the red couch week after week and Michael continued to tic, Carol didn't seem to mind.

I also felt comforted by Carol's presence. Her one-on-one attention and the homework she assigned kept Michael on track in almost every subject. I suspected he was falling behind in Spanish—the teacher rarely sent assignments or homework—but I didn't reach out because I was satisfied with his progress in math and English. It was something I would later regret.

As I switched on the car ignition, I put my peanut butter and jelly sandwich on the seat next to me, inserted my coffee in the cupholder, and reached for my fix: the chocolate bar stashed in my purse. I remember thinking that it could be worse—I could be reaching for booze.

Next, I chose a CD from my console. Two summers before, Russ and I had hosted a Woodstock 40th anniversary party in our backyard. Usually, I started my drive listening to three CDs we had burned, titled Woodstock 1, 2, and 3. The '60s-era music, like The Grateful Dead's "Sugar Magnolia," or Janis Joplin's "Bobby McGee," which my neighbor had sung at our party, brought me back to a happier time.

When I was in my car, alone, with my playlist, I was in my happy place, at least until I hit a traffic jam. As I sat there in that line of cars, nibbling chocolate, my thoughts turned to Michael, and soon I was wailing along with Janis, wondering if our son would ever get better. The week before, Russ had gently suggested that crying excessively in front of Michael and Katie was not a good idea. I agreed and had been trying to rein it in. I knew my role was to be a rock, to act stoic, as the therapist had suggested. So lately, I'd been trying to hold in my tears until I was alone in the car, maybe not the safest strategy.

Crying so much left me exhausted and wishing I could go to a hotel and sleep for a few weeks to escape my life. I imagined lying on clean white sheets, listless, drained of my superpowers like Superman after Kryptonite.

In reality, I tried to keep up a normal family routine, cooking real dinners rather than serving up mac 'n' cheese on repeat. I made sure to read to Katie every night and give her some extra cuddling time. I kept my true feelings, the dark and doom-filled ones, to myself.

But I wondered how long I could sustain the act, playing the positive, upbeat, encouraging mom until we found something, anything, that would make Michael's tics subside. And I worried that I would run out of the energy necessary to continue what had become my vocation, my obsession. At the best of times, I'm not exactly a high-energy person. I like to joke that my idea of exercise is reading fast.

Now, I was pretending to be Supermom: working, taking care of the kids, and trying to find a cure for a medical problem that was by all accounts incurable. I worried incessantly about what would become of Michael. I gave little thought to what would become of me.

When I pulled into the faculty parking lot, I popped another piece of chocolate into my mouth for fortification, then proceeded to put on another show, pretending to be the extrovert I wasn't, filling an hour and 15 minutes with thoughts on how to write a lede, fairness in journalism, and the importance of balanced reporting, with a dash of AP style thrown in. Still 12 weeks to go before the end of the semester.

On my commute home, I tended to listen to NPR instead of music; it was less emotional for me. I never knew exactly what I'd find when I got home: the old Michael, my cheerful, mischievous boy, or the new, ticcing, post-diagnosis Michael, whose up-and-down emotions often scared and saddened me.

On this day, Michael was with my mother-in-law, Helga, who took over when Carol left. Helga is a graphic artist by training, and the two of them had started on an Ancestry.com project, including drawing a detailed family tree. Except for the tics that still came in spurts but were a bit less frequent, Michael's life had gotten very quiet. No school. No chorus practice. His one weekly outing was to a therapist. Michael hated therapy, but we continued in part because it seemed like a necessity, given the situation. Despite the occasional outbursts, there was still joy in Michael's life; besides playing games and watching the *Lord of the Rings* trilogy over and over, he took a real interest in a variety of projects, like the family tree, sometimes reminding me of a new retiree exploring various hobbies.

He also resumed drum and guitar lessons, which he had started a few years back but quit shortly thereafter. I had emailed his instructors after he began ticcing in January, and now they were both giving him weekly lessons. I noticed he was playing on his own more, sitting in the basement trying his hand at some songs by Green Day, his new favorite band.

Why would he want to go back to school?

Michael's main source of excitement was watching *American Idol*, a family favorite since the show had begun 10 seasons earlier. That February, we were more invested than usual, all of us enamored with a 21-year-old contestant named James Durbin, a standout from the beginning with his high-pitched tenor and funky California vibe. He played guitar. He was cool. He was young—and he happened to have Tourette syndrome. *What were the odds?*

While he spoke, Durbin blinked and squeaked and scrunched up his face like a child swallowing a nasty spoonful of medicine. But when he sang, he stopped ticcing, as if a switch had been turned off in his brain. In his audition, Durbin wore a leather-fringed vest over a bright green shirt, a scarf dangling from his back like a tail. Shyly, he asked Aerosmith's Steven Tyler, one of the *Idol* judges, if he could sing one of Tyler's songs. Then he launched into "Dream On"—a cappella.

During the performance, Steven Tyler closed his eyes and rocked his head in approval, and fellow judge Jennifer Lopez cried.

"*Wow. Man*, that was over the top. So, so good," said Tyler.

"When I was younger, I was diagnosed with Tourette," Durbin told the judges after the performance. "But when I sing, it just all goes away. I don't have a care in the world."

Every Wednesday night, the four of us sat on the red couch in the living room, rooting for the cool kid with Tourette as he crooned his way into a chance at winning the top prize. Though Michael didn't say much when James Durbin was performing, I knew he dreamed of trying out for the show someday.

Durbin clearly had not been cured of Tourette, but he was managing it enough to be able to function—and even soar. I think watching him during that difficult time gave all of us hope that even if Michael never stopped ticcing, he might at least gain the confidence to live a somewhat normal life.

Watching James Durbin was the first time I truly understood that I needed to accept Michael the way he was and help him to do the same. I remember thinking, *Maybe this young man will give Michael the shred of confidence he needs. Maybe he'll show Michael that even if he has Tourette, he could someday perform on stage. Maybe, one day, it will be Michael who doesn't have a care in the world.*

In addition to connecting Michael to drum and guitar teachers, I'd also found a singer who did mind/body work. Her name was Anitra Brooks, and both kids had met her a few years back at a theater camp they attended. She started working with Michael soon after he began ticcing, and when they went down to our basement, I could hear soothing music accompanied by a drum, played by Michael.

After the first meeting, Anitra told me that Michael didn't tic as much when he was drumming. I didn't give her comment much thought, though I had read that tics tend to improve when a child is focused on an activity, whether it's playing a musical instrument or swinging a baseball bat.

Then, a month later, on a long car ride to Vermont during winter break, Michael pulled out his drumsticks and began drumming on the back of the driver's seat as we blasted everything from the Beatles ("Oh! Darling") to Queen ("Somebody to Love" and "Bohemian Rhapsody"). Despite the volume of the music, the car suddenly seemed quiet: Michael's incessant ticcing had stopped. After a few more similar experiences, we were pretty sure that playing music was a balm that could quell his tics.

I was excited and intrigued, as was Russ. It seemed mysterious to both of us, but so was everything about Tourette.

In the past, Michael had never been too diligent about practicing, and he had never even learned a full song, instead playing chords to "Smoke on the Water" and "Seven Nation Army" over and over. But now he wasn't in school, and Carol came for only two hours a day. I wasn't sure if it was due to *American Idol* or boredom, but his interest in playing instruments appeared to be turning into a passion. Looking back, it seems more like fate.

I could tell that Michael enjoyed all the music in his life—the sessions with Anitra and his music lessons. And I was thrilled that music seemed to quiet his tics. But I considered it a temporary fix. I didn't connect the dots and think music could be therapeutic in a more substantial way—that maybe it could even heal him.

Still, when I realized that Michael had a concert coming up with his school choir—at Carnegie Hall, no less, an event where other choirs from schools joined in—I urged him to participate.

As a younger boy, Michael had tried soccer, T-ball, and other sports, but none of them had stuck. I signed him up for karate because I'd read that it can help kids become more disciplined and gain self-control, not to mention build self-esteem. But one of the only extracurricular activities he seemed to enjoy was singing in the school's honor choir, an audition-only group. How I concluded that it was a good idea to allow Michael to perform onstage a mere six weeks after he started ticcing is a mystery to me. Maybe I saw it as a test to see if he could handle being around other kids, even briefly. Michael surprised me by agreeing; he must have been bored after being holed up at home for more than a month. The choir director also thought it was a good idea, despite the fact that Michael had missed so many practices.

Thankfully, the concert was on February 27, during what seemed to be an extended lull in Michael's ticcing. I had read that tics waxed and waned, and Michael's definitely fluctuated in frequency, though not severity, at this point, coming and going on their own schedule. We could not figure out any rhyme or reason as to why they would suddenly stop and then reappear out of nowhere.

But this lull was the longest so far, lasting a good 10 days, and I was all jazzed up, hoping and praying that the Tenex was starting to work even though he had been taking it for only a month. I let myself believe that maybe the worst was over. Which is how Russ, Helga, Katie, and I found ourselves in New York City, sitting in Carnegie Hall's plush red velvet chairs, waiting for the concert to begin.

Michael, like all the other children, was dressed in a red vest and black pants, but I had no trouble picking him out when the choir filed onto the stage. With his thick mane of brown hair swept to the side, he looked like a slightly plump, prepubescent Justin Bieber. Michael had been impressed when I told him that the Beatles had performed at the same storied venue. But as we waited for the concert to begin, a wave of dread began rising in my stomach. I was fairly certain that I was the only mother ever to sit in the audience at Carnegie Hall and wonder if her child would drop the F-bomb from the stage, which would surely resound in the 2,800-seat music hall known for its perfect acoustics.

Thankfully, there were 300 kids onstage besides Michael, all of them part of the National Children's Chorus, including 61 students from our town, every one of them silent (for the moment), calm, and serious-looking. My body was tense until the children began to sing Mozart's *Missa Brevis No. 1*. As soon as I heard the first note, the sweet childish voices singing, a wave of emotion washed over me, the performers a blur of red vests through my tears. I can't remember much about that concert, but I'll never forget what I was thinking: *Our ordeal is finally over. Michael is better.*

Then, after the performance, as the kids were milling around, Michael looked at me and said, "Bitch!" in a voice loud enough for a boy in his class to hear. Even that couldn't puncture the buoyant sense of relief I felt as I walked Michael to the Hard Rock Cafe, where a dinner was planned for the kids in the choir and their chaperones. The Hard Rock, with its electric atmosphere and loud rock music, was the perfect cover if Michael ticced. As I watched him from across the room, sitting at a table with his classmates, talking and laughing, our life felt almost normal for the first time in six weeks.

Later that night, I asked Michael how he had liked being with his friends again, performing and going out to dinner, at the Hard Rock Cafe, no less. He didn't say much, but it was the happiest I had seen him in weeks.

Two days later, Michael started ticcing again—almost as violently as he had on day one. I took little comfort in the fact that we'd be going back to Yale in a few days. Instead, I ran into the bedroom and shouted a stream of curses into my pillow. I, too, had begun cursing by then, intentionally and often.

Chapter 9

Throwing Spaghetti at the Wall

When we arrived at Dr. Sukhodolsky's office at Yale, he was eager to tell us about the trial he was conducting on CBIT as a possible treatment for Tourette. Adolescents enrolled in the study would attend eight sessions over 10 weeks where they would be trained to control activity in a region of their brain associated with premonitory urges to tic. That urge has been described as "discomfort," an "energy," and an "alarm in the brain."

As Dr. Sukhodolsky enthusiastically explained how researchers on his team would teach Michael to do a competing behavior like smacking his lips instead of cursing, it was clear he hoped that Michael would agree to be in the trial. Part of the doctor's excitement was that during the previous year, 2010, a large, multi-center study had been published in the *Journal of the American Medical Association*

(*JAMA*) showing that CBIT was more effective than standard therapy for reducing tics in children and adults. More than half of the kids enrolled in the study had "clinically significant" improvements in their tics, which was considered a major breakthrough in the treatment of Tourette.

But I was feeling a bit miffed, barely able to take in the doctor's words. Early on in the appointment, as I was bringing Dr. S. up to speed, he had turned to Michael—who was cursing a blue streak as usual—and said, plainly, "You have to go back to school."

"He can't go back yet," I said. "We are going to wait until he tics less."

"Nothing happens overnight," he replied. "He has to go back to school."

I bit the inside of my mouth, but only because I didn't want to risk offending the only person who might be able to help us. Of course, he was just one of the many medical professionals who urged me to get Michael back into school. Thinking about it now, I know that he was well-meaning and that there are plenty of reasons why kids with tics should not be isolated at home.

Before the meeting was over, he repeated his edict at least three more times. *Nobody wants Michael back in school more than I do*, I thought. *But there's no way he's ready.*

Then came the clincher: Dr. Sukhodolsky looked at Michael and said, "If you enroll in the trial, we will pay you $20 per visit."

I was a bit surprised by this, but I would later learn that it's not uncommon to pay research subjects as an incentive for participating in medical research.

Michael smiled as if someone had said—well, that they were going to give him 20 bucks every week for 10 weeks.

"That's $200," Michael said, the first non-curse words he had said during the appointment.

"We'll also pay you $50 for donating blood."

As Michael daydreamed about how he would spend his windfall, I asked more questions.

To my mind, there were several problems with this plan. First, it would require ten trips to Yale in the coming months—at least an hour's drive each way. I was also dismayed to learn that though CBIT could be effective, it might take months for Michael to master the technique. From my research, I also knew that it would take hard work and commitment. Ten weeks would bring us to mid-May—nearly the end of the school year. Surely the meds would have kicked in by then and we'd be free of this.

Despite my reservations, I booked an appointment for Michael's initial assessment. The only available weekly slot was at 5 o'clock on a Friday night, at the height of rush hour, meaning I'd have to leave two hours, not one, to get there, and that Katie would either have to tag along or be left with friends for several hours, then and on every Friday after school.

But it wasn't only the commute. I would have driven to Florida if I thought it would cure Michael. I wasn't convinced that Michael would do the exercises diligently—or that they would work.

Dr. Sukhodolsky had told us that during one part of the study, they would monitor Michael's brain waves while he donned a space-age bathing cap embedded with electrodes. Michael thought it sounded cool, but I was wary about my son being a guinea pig, particularly for something that would only control—and not cure—his symptoms.

What I wanted was for my child to return to his pre-Tourette state, or, better yet, develop into an improved version who would realize his potential in every way possible. What I wanted was a miracle.

One of the appealing aspects of the study was that we might begin to understand what occurred in the brain of a kid with Tourette—the sequence of events that led to a tic. Dr. Coffman, of Children's Mercy Kansas City, later explained it to me this way: "The basal ganglia, a group of paired structures near the center of the brain, are...like the braking system of the brain. When the body goes to make a movement, this system makes sure the movements that come out are the ones you want to come out," he described. "In patients with Tourette, the brakes are leaky, so extra movement signals manage to escape from the basal ganglia, then show up in basic patterns of movement where they are not supposed to be. That's how tics come to be: They escape through the braking system."

He added that this was why, when you look at people who tic, it looks for the most part like a movement they might do naturally; it doesn't appear atypical or abnormal until it happens so frequently that it catches your eye.

After Russ and I discussed it, we reluctantly decided to take a pass on participating in the study (although Michael did donate blood and got $50). Instead, I decided I would look for an expert in CBIT based closer to home.

I am not sure I would have made the same decision had I known that in a decade, CBIT would become an effective first-line treatment for Tourette, partly due to the researchers' work at Yale. "The recommendation we are currently offering is to do behavioral treatments first," Dr. Leckman told me in 2023. "We actually avoid the use of medications unless we need to go down that road."

By the time we arrived home that afternoon, I'd already decided to change tack and explore a few of the alternative treatments I'd read about. I couldn't wait for mainstream medicine or research results; I was a mom on a mission and in a hurry.

Before I knew it, I had fallen down an Internet rabbit hole, scrolling sites that listed possible Tourette triggers, such as vaccines, cleaning products, mold, and even dairy products and chocolate. Less common culprits included certain medications, chlorine (did that mean he could never go in a pool again?!), new carpeting, paint and paint thinners, and pesticides. Even video games purportedly prompted tics.

I thought, *Michael eats dairy and chocolate. My house has its share of dust. Could our renovation have caused this?* In short order, I was obsessing over everything Michael ate and any medicine he took or vaccines he'd received that could have led to the condition. Was it a spider bite? Mold in the basement? Allergies?

But when Russ, Michael, and I met with an allergist in New York City to explore this latter theory, he didn't have the answers I craved. Instead, he demonstrated what may have happened: "See this?" he said, as he grabbed a mug on his desk stuffed with two dozen or so pens and pencils. "There was your home renovation and the transition to middle school and his social life.... It just came to a boil and overflowed, like this mug!"

My job was to get things back to a simmer.

While the allergist's colorful analogy was helpful, it still did not answer the pressing question: What causes Tourette? The words *stress*, *excitement*, and *anxiety* kept popping up, something I remembered years later when the Covid-19 pandemic hit. In the spring of 2020, just after the pandemic began, teenagers worldwide began to develop intense, complex motor tics—like hitting, whistling, and whooping, often after watching videos on Instagram or TikTok of people who said they had Tourette. Videos tagged #tourettes had more than 5 billion views by the summer of 2022—up from 1.25 billion in January of that year.

Major media outlets, including *The Wall Street Journal,* covered the story. When I first read about the phenomenon, I was curious—and skeptical—because you can't "catch" Tourette syndrome from watching other people tic on social media. But experts I spoke with explained that most of these teens likely didn't have Tourette. Instead, the TikTok ticcers, as they came to be known, had developed a type of functional neurological disorder (FND). In this instance, the group with FND included teens—mostly girls—whose brains subconsciously generated tics while watching Tourette videos. When I asked Dr. Coffman about it, he blamed increased consumption of social media during Covid as one of the main factors. "But it's clear that the movements are in no way consistent with Tourette because they are so incredibly dramatic and unusual."

Functional tic-like behaviors (FTLB), a subtype of FNDs, were relatively rare until the pandemic. The Rutgers University Tourette Syndrome Clinic witnessed a 97% increase in the number of referrals for teenage girls with tics starting in March 2020, and most of them had FTLBs, according to Dr. Graham Hartke, Psy.D., a psychologist and former director of the clinic.

He told me that the surge in FTLBs occurred during a wider mental health crisis affecting teenagers across the country, and that most of the affected teens had a history of anxiety and depression. Then came the stress of the pandemic combined with the increased use of social media featuring individuals showcasing extreme tic behaviors, which created the perfect storm FTLBs to develop. "All of a sudden you are doing something you have never done before, and it's scary," he said. "It's very disruptive and potentially traumatizing."

What I knew then was that I wanted to do something—anything—to reduce my son's anxiety. "Anything that increases relaxation or decreases anxiety will likely correspond with reduced tics at some point," Helene Walisever told me, recommending massage, yoga, and deep breathing, among other strategies. "Anything that helps a person feel more relaxed and in their body can't hurt."

So I took Michael to Jacques, the acupuncturist who was a friend and former colleague of Russ's. I did not truly grasp the concept of *qi*—defined as vital energy in Chinese medicine. But I put blind faith in Jacques because, a decade earlier, Russ had slipped and fallen on a dock when he was fishing and was so banged up he could barely move. He went to see Jacques for acupuncture and felt better within hours. But when Michael tried it, he hated it. What 11-year-old boy wants to be pricked with 20 needles and then left alone in a room for 20 minutes listening to New Age music?

None of the mainstream doctors we'd met with had mentioned complementary therapies, but I ordered the best-selling *Natural Treatments for Tics & Tourette's,* by Sheila Rogers DeMare, which spells out how to find and address Tourette triggers and lists a wide array of alternative therapies for Tourette. After skimming the book and reading a few articles online, I put Michael on a protocol of lecithin (a B vitamin) and fish oil, which had been shown to reduce tics in some kids and seemed fairly innocuous.

A few years later, DeMare would criticize the TAA for turning a blind eye to mounting evidence that alternative treatments for Tourette are effective. By 2022, *Tourette Syndrome,* the textbook co-edited by Dr. Leckman and Dr. Davide Martino that compiles expertise from around the world, had an entire chapter titled "Complementary and Integrative Health Medicine in Tourette Syndrome," which chronicles the growing body of evidence to support these treatments.

The outcome was less positive for me. Basically, I became suspicious of everything, my paranoia stoked by online forums that sucked me in like quicksand, full of despairing mothers like me who were trying to unearth the cause of their child's suffering. Some, like me, also worried that they were somehow responsible.

Russ, for his part, was a bit wary of my inquiries. Despite embracing complementary therapies in his practice, one of his pet peeves was patients who'd gotten medical information from sites that were not credible, then showed up in his office with an incorrect self-diagnosis in hand. As a journalist, I was all too aware of the pitfalls of my grab-bag approach to Tourette treatments. There was a sharp distinction between the content posted on sites like the TAA or articles penned by medical doctors and the information I perused on less credentialed sites, often written by people grasping at straws, feeling lost and alone and afraid. Like me.

But the posts also represented something in short supply in our lives: hope. It helped me to feel that I was not the only parent in this predicament. This community of parents sharing information and cheering for the successes of other members was uplifting. Like me, they weren't entirely satisfied with the wait-and-see response from mainstream medicine and seemed intent on finding their own remedies.

To my credit, I did not follow up on a few fringe recommendations, like the one for a New Jersey doctor who charged $3,000 up front just to walk in the door for an initial assessment. Her signature treatment was long-term intravenous antibiotics.

I did, however, research marijuana as a possible treatment after reading an article in *The New York Times* about a study that showed improvement in Tourette patients after using cannabis. The experts cited were none other than Dr. King and Dr. Leckman — the renowned Yale doctors. This was 2010, two years before Colorado became the first state to legalize recreational marijuana; it would be a few more years before the zeitgeist shifted and marijuana use was decriminalized in many states and used frequently to treat Tourette.

Back then I wondered, *At what age is using pot OK? Once he's past puberty, could I call an old college friend who still smokes and ask for a bag?* I didn't pursue the idea further, but I kept it in my back pocket, kind of like an inside joke—with myself.

"Happy 18th birthday, kiddo! Here's a pipe and some weed!"

Thoughts like these made me smile and were part of the new inner dialogue running continuously through my mind like a never-ending ticker tape.

Meanwhile, I continued to meticulously chart Michael's symptoms in my notebook, which was filled with columns listing the date of any medical interventions we tried and Michael's resulting symptoms. I didn't realize that trying so many things at once would make it impossible to know what was helping and what wasn't. But I was throwing spaghetti at a wall and seeing what stuck.

Every time we visited a new doctor, I was convinced that they would be the miracle worker Michael needed. Never mind that our health insurance didn't cover many of these nonstandard therapies. Most of the people we saw took credit cards. Whether we could pay the bills when they arrived was a problem for another day.

Sometimes I thought my efforts were working, especially during the periods where Michael's tics waned before they came roaring back. Though I sometimes question whether all my desperate, disparate attempts made a difference, I'm not the type of mother who could have watched and waited to see if things turned out OK. I was not always confident in my ability to help my son, but I was like a dog with a bone: *I'm not letting go until I figure this out.* I wouldn't settle for being a "good-enough mother"—the term British pediatrician and psychoanalyst Donald Winnicott coined in the 1950s to deter mothers from seeking perfection in their parenting, which can backfire. Instead, I took to heart something Jackie Kennedy once said: "If you bungle raising your children, I don't think whatever else you do matters very much."

Fortunately, I eventually found a lively, personable, positive guy who was an MD and had also trained in complementary medicine. Plus, he took our insurance. He told us about a promising study reported in the prestigious British medical journal *The Lancet*. It suggested that kids with ADHD—which many kids with Tourette also have—might benefit from something known as the elimination diet, which involved taking pretty much every type of enticing food off the table to help the body "eliminate or clear various toxins."

That meant Michael had to stop eating beef, pork, veal, dairy, most grains (wheat, oats, corn), and sugar. Maybe the kids who outgrew Tourette had all become gluten-free vegans?

I had already read about the connection between diet and tics, and there was an entire chapter in the DeMare book devoted to the topic. Foods that purportedly caused negative neurological reactions included milk, eggs, dairy, chocolate, beef—all staples in our family's diet. Of course, chemical additives, processed foods, and pesticides were also on the "no" list, and there were also reports that sugar could trigger tics.

This wasn't something Michael would like, but I was intrigued.

"Let's give it a try," I said, optimistic again. After all, Russ and I had once tried a vegan diet detox, and the results were amazing. When it was over, I had lost 11 pounds, and Russ had lost 17 pounds. Better yet, my skin was clear, and I felt like a sexy, speedy sports car that had had a tune-up. Of course, we had to endure it for only three weeks, whereas the protocol Michael was on might last months.

The next day, Michael and I went to a local supermarket and filled our cart with approved groceries like millet, quinoa, and organic vegetables and fruits. So far, so good, until we got to the checkout counter, and a young woman greeted us at the cash register.

"Hello, how are you?" she said. The store prided itself on service, and the clerks were particularly cheerful.

I froze.

Michael had been ticcing a lot in the store, but since the aisles were rarely packed with people, I thought it would be a safe outing for him.

"Did you find everything OK?"

"Yes," I said. Michael was quiet, but I knew there was no telling what might set him off—and that seeing a cashier who was Black could prompt him to say that word. Grabbing the bags, stuffing them with groceries, I hustled us out of the store so fast that I was certain the woman thought I must have kidnapped Michael and threatened to harm him if he spoke.

When I got home, I tried to make a meal plan, surveying the grains now stowed in our pantry: brown rice, millet, quinoa, amaranth, and buckwheat. I had never cooked with any of these except brown rice. Michael's favorite breakfast cereal, Quaker Oatmeal Squares, was off-limits, and I couldn't make a turkey sandwich because cold cuts and bread were also forbidden. I began experimenting with these new ingredients, with some successes and some epic fails (buckwheat, for example, turned out to be something everybody in the family despised).

By day three, with Michael still not thrilled about the new diet, I decided to make a gluten-free, sugar-free, dairy-free cake. When I took the finished product out of the oven, half of it deflated, and it resembled a sandcastle that had been torpedoed by a wave. After dinner, we tasted it. Nobody took more than one bite. Michael walked away from the table.

That didn't stop me. As a show of support for Michael, I decided to try the diet with him. After all, I had told him, over and over, "We'll get through this *together*."

Except when Michael wasn't around, I cheated, putting sugar and milk in my coffee, sneaking in bites of cheese and crackers, and hiding my wineglass behind the coffeepot. I didn't give up my secret chocolate habit, and I'd added a new treat, Nutella—the crack cocaine of chocolate lovers—which I hid in a cupboard.

Then, after five already challenging days, we faced the biggest challenge yet: My mother came to visit. As usual, she brought a list of meals she intended to make, ones she'd planned weeks in advance. Pasta, breaded veal cutlets, and homemade chocolate chip cookies were just a few of her staples.

When she learned about the diet, it was as if I had told her that Michael and I had decided to become atheists.

"What will I cook?"

Then she began to cry.

That's when I knew our experiment was over.

I went to the store and bought the ingredients for fettuccine Alfredo: butter, ricotta, Parmesan, sour cream, and pasta. I am not sure I have ever seen Michael happier.

Chapter 10

A Date, a Dog, and a Drug

The week after the Carnegie Hall concert, I received a call from Michael's guidance counselor.

"We need Michael to come in next week to take the CMTs," she told me, referring to the statewide Connecticut Mastery Test, nicknamed "children's mental torture" by the students. I was no fan either.

"He can't come to school," I said. "He can't be in a room with other students."

"He needs to take the CMTs," the guidance counselor repeated. "We can put him in a room with other students who are allowed accommodations."

This was the first time I had heard the word *accommodations* used in this context. She was referring to students who qualified for special education services and were given allowances such as extra time on tests.

86

"I still don't think that will work," I said, trying to be polite, adding, "It will be uncomfortable for him because he still makes lots of sounds and even words," I said. "And it will be very disruptive for the other kids."

I could just picture it: Michael shouting obscenities in a room set aside for kids who needed a quiet space to concentrate. Why didn't this person get that my son wasn't in school because he couldn't be around other human beings?

I wanted to scream. Instead, I said, "I'll think about it." But I knew there was no way Michael could take that test. He was very self-conscious, especially in public, and his anxiety seemed to trigger a stream of curse words, though sometimes he was able to semi-suppress them, *fucks* and *shits* sounding more like "*fff*" and "*shh.*"

This was little comfort, since he was adding new words to his repertoire all the time. *Tits* and *douchebag* were the latest. Who knew what might happen while he was sitting in a room with other students?

"Hell will freeze over before I make him take a test that has no bearing on his education," I hissed on the phone to Russ. On I went, telling him what he already knew. "Michael has already missed six weeks of school due to a bizarre illness, and all they care about is the damn test, probably because he does well on these things." After I vented, I felt better.

"Fucking rookie," I said before we hung up. "There was not a hint of compassion in her voice."

Ten minutes later, the phone rang. The principal, Shelley Somers, was on the line.

"Michael can take the CMTs in my office. He'll be the only one there."

Although I opposed the school's emphasis on standardized testing, I was willing to compromise. On some level, I hoped that if I was conciliatory now, Michael might get some leeway from the school later.

Once Michael found out that he would be quarantined in the principal's office, he nervously agreed to go. And when we arrived at school the following week, the principal greeted him warmly. Two hours later, the receptionist called to say Michael was done with the test.

"How did it go?" I asked when I picked him up.

"Fine."

"Where'd you take the test?"

"In the principal's office."

"Was she nice?"

"Really nice."

"Did you tic?"

"Yes, but she didn't care."

It's a start, I thought.

The test would go on for two weeks, and every morning, I drove Michael to school and walked him inside to the principal's office. Michael continued to say he felt comfortable there, though walking away, I could often hear him shout "Bitch! Bitch!" through the closed door. But when I showed up at the end, the two of them were usually chatting casually.

"Michael told me all about your family, and the new dog you're getting," she said one day, referring to the puppy we had been looking into getting in the spring or summer. By then, we had picked out a dog from a litter in Vermont and had all begun discussing names. At night, Russ read chapters aloud from a dog training book so we could learn how to raise a well-behaved puppy.

"I feel like I'm part of the family," Shelley said. I hoped that she was right and that when he returned to school, he would have someone like family on his side.

Soon after, Shelley invited me in to talk. She said she couldn't be with Michael for the last two days of testing because she had to attend a conference, but an assistant principal would fill in. She added that she hoped Michael would return to school soon and that he was welcome to come to her office or the guidance counselor's office whenever he was ticcing or just needed a break. When we arrived for testing the next day, she had left a Hershey's Kiss the size of a tennis ball for Michael, along with a note. I was downright giddy—and optimistic that Michael would return to school even though, after a brief lull where he was able to muffle his tics, they were now back in full force.

Yet Michael remained adamant about not going back. He said he couldn't stop thinking about what the kids would say and think about why he had been absent. The truth is, word had started to get out. A friend whose daughter was also in sixth grade with Michael told me that "a bunch of girls are all concerned, and the drama is beginning to grow." I passed this on to Michael, who continued to hope that he could tell the kids he had mono or some other illness that would explain his long absence. Russ and I urged him to come clean, but he would have none of it.

One day, a girl called our home phone and I answered. I heard giggles and then a click. The next week, another girl called and asked for Michael, but he refused to take the call. She seemed genuinely concerned and told me someone had told her that Michael had Tourette syndrome, and that a bunch of girls at her lunch table were talking about it. Some kids emailed him, asking the same questions. He never responded, distressed to know that his secret was out.

I remember thinking that if and when he did go back, lots of attention from the girls in the sixth grade might be good for him. Meanwhile, on a day-to-day basis, other than the two hours of tutoring, and visits from my mother-in-law, it was mostly up to me to keep Michael engaged and occupied.

Michael and I played more Hangman and watched hours of *Cake Boss*, a reality TV show featuring a New Jersey baker whose extended Italian family reminded both of us of my family. Eventually, we even visited the bakery featured on the show.

One day, Michael made up a board game he called Fork in the Road, in which players were graded based on various behaviors as they traveled around the makeshift board. The demerit cards included:

"Spit milk through nose at lunch while laughing." Go back to Grade: 1.

"Surprise B.O. appears." Grade: 2.

"Accidentally fart in math class." Grade: 2 (and go to detention).

"Steal girlfriend from BF." Grade: 1.

"Get 'pantsed' at school." Roll dice.

As for the positive cards, which Michael dubbed EZ Pass, these included:

"Join the soccer team." Grade: 1.

"Pool party." Grade: 3.

"Mow a senior citizen's lawn." Grade: 1.

"New lead singer in band." Grade: 2.

"Acne resolved." Grade: 1.

The game made me laugh and gave me insight into the mind of an 11-year-old boy who was bored and clearly needed to be around people under the age of 45. I was happy that our bond was deepening, but I also worried that my son was becoming too dependent on me.

By March, two months after Michael's ticcing began, he no longer seemed antsy or agitated. Instead, he had become complacent and even cheerful, settling into a routine like an adult who had gotten laid off and then begun relishing the free time, not worried about finding a new job. I was making food he liked, spending lots of time alone with him, and, in truth, maybe spoiling him a bit. My life, our family life, revolved around him completely, at least during the day.

Meanwhile, I continued to brainstorm. *What if Michael took a low dose of Xanax to get him to relax enough to go back?* I had begun taking half a dose of Xanax (alprazolam) a few times a week when I was feeling on edge. I still cried almost daily, sometimes in front of the kids, though I tried to escape to the bathroom when I felt the tears coming. But half a Xanax did wonders. The drug is a benzodiazepine used to treat anxiety and panic disorders—a quick fix as opposed to a long-term solution. Russ was never a huge proponent (*he* never needed drugs), but all I cared about at the time was that it felt soothing, like drinking a Bloody Mary at noon.

I wondered if a tiny dose would help make it easier for Michael to go back to school in person. Russ said the pediatrician wouldn't agree because Xanax could be addictive.

I called her anyway. "I've been taking Xanax and was wondering if it's something we could prescribe for Michael if it's safe for kids. He weighs almost as much as I do."

"How much do you take?" she asked.

"My prescription is for 0.25 milligrams, but I cut the pill in half."

She laughed. "That's a subclinical dose!" Then, as Russ had warned, she explained that doctors typically do not prescribe Xanax or similar antianxiety drugs to minors because they can be addictive.

Then something serendipitous happened: Katie ran into the girl who had called to check on Michael, who asked if Michael was going to the sixth-grade social. When Katie got home, she relayed the question to Michael in front of me.

"You should go!" I said.

He looked interested, and skeptical.

"I think your friends miss you," Katie said. "You should go."

Bless her, my 9-year-old is the most emotionally astute person in the house, I thought. She had more or less stayed quiet about Michael's predicament, but I think she chimed in because she felt the girl genuinely cared.

"What if they ask where I've been? What if they ask what's wrong with me?"

"It might not come up," I said. "Just go and have fun."

"I don't want to go alone," he said.

91

I have to get him to that dance! I thought, wishing for a fairy god-mother like the one who waved her wand and whisked Cinderella off to attend the royal ball.

I don't remember if Katie or I suggested that he go with the girl who'd asked about him, but he emailed her that night, and the next day, he told me he would go to the dance. For the next week, I felt like a woman planning her wedding after going on a first date, except my hope was that Michael's attending the dance would lead to his returning to school.

The day of the dance, April Fool's Day, I kept thinking, *The joke is going to be on me if he reneges!* But that night, Michael and I drove to the girl's house to pick her up, and I strained to listen to their soft chatter in the back seat. When we arrived, I got out of the car with them. I had agreed to be a chaperone at the dance—I didn't intend to miss this—but I made sure to trail well behind them as they approached the side door of the gymnasium.

Michael and his friend went inside, and from the doorway, I could see a scrum of kids standing around. Once they spotted Michael, though, it was as if they'd seen a celebrity. I watched as a dozen boys and girls rushed over, swarming around Michael, hugging him and talking excitedly. Michael had always claimed he didn't have many friends, and I didn't recognize most of the kids in the group, but I didn't care. They were his friends tonight.

For the next two hours, I watched as my son danced to Katy Perry and Bruno Mars, a smile plastered on his face. The ticcing was not noticeable at all. I remember thinking, *I need to send that girl a thank you note because she changed his life.*

But the next day, when I suggested we contact the guidance coun-selor to arrange for him to go back to school, Michael refused. He had fun, he said, but attending school was still out of the question.

~

A few days later, the two of us drove to Vermont to pick up our new dog—a Golden Retriever. We had a hard time finding the house, and I kept driving up and down the same winding country road until we finally pulled into a driveway. We knew we were in the right spot when we saw half a dozen Golden Retrievers roaming the expansive backyard alongside cows and sheep. Inside, the breeder handed us a tiny, fluffy puppy the color of autumn leaves. Michael immediately took her in his arms and pet her lovingly.

When Michael and I talk about that trip now, he still gets choked up. "I remember that it was raining and how, when we walked inside, we were greeted by a dozen puppies. I don't think I'd ever been happier."

I felt the same. It was nothing short of love at first sight.

I had been reluctant to get a dog, but I finally gave in, telling the kids (and Russ) that once the renovation was done, we could look into it. On the way home, Michael sat in the backseat, cradling Bailey (a name Katie chose) on his lap as if he had been waiting for this day forever. When I saw the puppy in my son's arms, I knew I had made the right decision.

Bailey brought added chaos to our home, but having a puppy also gave Michael a job, getting him out of the house as he played with the puppy in the backyard and took her on short walks in the neighborhood. She was a welcome distraction.

Research has shown that interacting with pets can help autistic kids, and a few studies have shown that therapy dogs can reduce some of the symptoms of ADHD. And bringing a pet into the home of a child has long been thought to reduce stress and anxiety. It was also a companion for a kid stuck at home. Russ and I also thought it would be a great way to teach both our kids responsibility.

Although I have not found any studies on Tourette and pets, I didn't need a double-blind clinical trial to prove what I saw every day: Bailey was the best form of therapy we had found so far.

That said, she was not a panacea. Michael was still ticcing a lot, and as much as he said he wanted to stay home, he was becoming restless. At times, he seemed despondent, despite the new puppy. But his tics had gotten so bad—and even more profane, if that was possible—that I emailed Dr. King to ask if we should increase Michael's dose of Tenex. I also asked if he would prescribe a low dose of an antidepressant, explaining that we had noticed that Michael seemed increasingly anxious and depressed, which led to more ticcing. I hoped it would lessen his symptoms and dull his pain until I found the real antidote.

I knew Dr. King would probably bring up the subject of trying an antipsychotic drug like Risperdal. Before we showed up for the appointment, I did a deep dive on the Internet to learn about the medication. Several studies showed it was safe and effective for treating kids with Tourette, helping to tame the tics, though it wasn't approved by the FDA for that use. (The FDA approved Risperdal in 1993 to treat schizophrenia, bipolar disorder, and irritability in people with autism.) Dr. King later pointed out that Risperdal and other antipsychotics are more commonly referred to as neuroleptics because they are used off-label to treat many problems besides psychosis, including Tourette.

Still, the litany of potential side effects included increased cholesterol levels, dry mouth, and diarrhea. There were also a few less common but more troubling side effects like difficulty speaking or swallowing, a sudden inability to move the eyes, trembling fingers and hands, and involuntary twisting body movements that sounded as bad as the tics themselves.

And then there were the *rare* side effects: speech problems; sudden weakness or numbness in the face, arms, or legs; fast, weak heartbeat; pale, clammy skin; and something called *tardive dyskinesia*, which could cause involuntary—and irreversible—convulsions and spasms. In his book *Your Child in the Balance*, which is mostly about how to weigh the risks and benefits of prescription medications for children,

Dr. Kalikow included a chapter entitled "The Risks of Medicine." In it, he refers to LIV—lethal, irreversible, and very painful side effects. "Potentially irreversible side effects, though not life-threatening, also keep me awake," he wrote. He later told me, "I wrote that chapter for precisely what you were going through as a parent. It's not that you don't use these medicines. It's just that those are the ones that you ask, 'Does the benefit really merit that risk?'"

On the other hand, Dr. King later pointed out that there are potential risks of foregoing an effective treatment out of excessive caution, and that time is of the essence. "Symptoms aren't just bothersome in the here and now, but they have a cumulative debilitating effective, because they could be missing out on normal childhood development," he said. "You are potentially missing out on irrevocable opportunities to build self-esteem, acquire athletic skills or academic achievements, and develop peer relationships."

Another worry was that the medication could cause weight gain, and Michael was already self-conscious about his extra weight. Then there were my two personal favorites—"rapid or worm-like movements of the tongue" and something called *gynecomastia,* which in my mind, meant developing breasts like a sumo wrestler. I had a vision of my beautiful brown-haired boy growing thick around the middle along with an unwelcome pair of man boobs.

Russ and I were on the same page: The risks of Michael taking such a powerful drug still felt too great, at least for now.

When we met in person, Dr. King mentioned a newer drug called Geodon (ziprasidone), used primarily to treat schizophrenia and bipolar disorder. It did not cause weight gain. He also reassured me that all of the side effects I was obsessing over were "very rare."

As I sat in his office scribbling in my notebook, I caught on to something. Dr. King kept saying, "Our studies have shown..." I realized that some of the studies he was referring to were done at Yale under his and his colleagues' direction. I had been reluctant to put my trust in pharmaceuticals, given the risks to my child, but this news gave me confidence.

I asked, "How many patients have you seen with tardive dyskinesia?"

"None," he said. "That is, none in a child with Tourette on this medication for a reasonable amount of time."

When I asked how long it would take Geodon to start working, he said about a month.

It was a now-or-never moment: I knew that if Michael didn't return to school before summer break, he might refuse to go in the fall. He might never get his life back, which meant none of us would.

I turned to Russ. "I'm willing to try it...what do you think?"

He agreed. Even Michael seemed fine with it.

Russ had come to the appointment without my prodding, and now he and Dr. King launched into a detailed discussion about dosage. Russ explained that he could call a pharmacist he worked with to compound, or blend, the medicine to create a 5-milligram dose, instead of the usual 10 milligrams. We wanted to start Michael on the lowest dose possible, and 5-milligram tablets were not available through most pharmacies. The cost would be about $200 a month, and though Russ and I still argued about all of the money I had thrown at this problem—thousands of dollars by now—we agreed that this treatment was worth trying.

Chapter 11

Back to School?

Once we got Michael on the Geodon, I optimistically began preparing for his return to school and getting in touch with educator Fayne Molloy, recommended by the TAA. Molloy, they said, would help me navigate the system now that Michael had a diagnosis. Best of all, her services were free.

Molloy said Michael should have a 504 Plan in place before he returned to the classroom. A 504 Plan refers to Section 504 of the Rehabilitation Act of 1973, a federal law that prohibits discrimination against individuals with disabilities of any kind. The goal of the law is to ensure that schools remove barriers to learning for kids with disabilities, defined as "a physical or mental impairment that substantially limits one or more major life activities." I knew Michael would qualify because Tourette was deemed a disability in 2001. But I didn't know what should be included in Michael's 504 Plan, which could encompass everything from extended time on tests to reduced homework.

I learned I would have to work with the school to develop appropriate *accommodations*—there was that word again. Fayne Molloy explained that for someone like Michael, with uncontrollable tics, the plan might allow him to leave class if he had to and go to a designated area where an adult would be present.

By law, school districts are mandated to pay for a "free and appropriate education," even if it means paying for a private school if the district is unable to provide the services the student needs. But, as I would discover, that doesn't mean parents don't have to jump through hoops to actually secure those services for their children.

I wondered if Michael might also need an IEP (Individualized Education Plan), which would provide a lot more muscle than a 504 Plan, spelling out specific and measurable goals for helping kids learn and holding schools to them. IEPs often include specialized instruction for kids too—in other words, they go beyond accommodations like preferential seating in the classroom and extended time on tests. In addition, all IEPs must include benchmarks and goals, and schools are required to monitor students' progress.

But getting an IEP can be like wrangling a ticket to the Super Bowl, I learned, at least in the town where we lived. Even before Michael's diagnosis, I had heard horror stories from friends about how difficult it could be to convince the school system that their child needed one, in part because they are funded by taxpayers. Since then, *inclusivity* has become a cultural buzzword, and great efforts have been made to make sure kids with special needs are integrated into mainstream classrooms rather than segregated. This trend more or less started in 2002, when the No Child Left Behind law was passed with great fanfare. Among many other things, the law supports the idea that students receiving specialized services be taught alongside their "typical" peers in a regular classroom.

"The ultimate goal is for students with Tourette, even those with obvious or noisy symptoms, to be integrated into the main classroom. If their peers are educated as to why a student [like Michael] is cursing or screeching, that can really diminish the social effects on him," Helene Walisever told me recently. "Once kids understand why someone is cursing or making whatever sounds, you'd be surprised at how it really becomes background noise."

But when I talked with Fayne Molloy about getting an IEP for Michael, she wasn't exactly encouraging. Ultimately, though, she agreed that his tics were so severe that it might be difficult for him to focus, and therefore excel, in a classroom setting without special accommodations. I later learned that 34% of kids diagnosed with Tourette syndrome also have some other sort of learning disability, according to the CDC. And in the 2020–21 TAA impact survey, 76% of parents said their child had an IEP.

I had actually inquired about an IEP for Michael back when he was getting in trouble in third grade. I was turned down then. But now that Michael had missed school for almost three months and had a bona fide medical diagnosis, I assumed, or at least hoped, that he would now be eligible.

With an IEP, Michael would have access to a resource room where he could go if he was ticcing, and a special education teacher would be in charge of his education instead of a guidance counselor (who is typically the point person for a 504 Plan). In other words, rather than hitting balls alone in the backyard, he would have a coach as he navigated the remainder of his middle school career.

That's what he needs—someone overseeing him inside the school building, I thought. *Someone who is on his side, other than his parents.*

Then there were the logistics of actually getting Michael back into the classroom. Fayne Molloy suggested he start back gradually, perhaps by meeting with the tutor in the school library to get him used to being in the building. "Go one day to start," she suggested.

"Try music, gym, and one academic class, and involve him in the decision-making." I thought these ideas were brilliant.

She also suggested that I ask a TAA representative to come talk to the entire sixth grade about Tourette. "The more the kids know, the better," she said. "And teachers too."

I nodded, assuming that most teachers would be extremely compassionate when it came to Michael's condition. Ideally, they would cut him some slack but not let him get away with too much.

I assumed a lot.

~

I explained the plan to Michael's new tutor, Richelle: First, she'd tutor Michael in the school building after hours, and his teachers would come by just to say hi. Then, when he was ready, he would move on to attend a couple of classes a day.

When we broached this plan with Michael in April, I only mentioned tutoring him in the school, after hours.

"Are you sure I wouldn't have to be around other kids?" he asked.

"Nope," I said. "We will wait until the buses pull out and sneak you right into the cafeteria."

Miraculously, he said yes, mostly because he would not see other kids and vice versa. Perhaps due to the Geodon, he could now suppress his tics enough so that he could take a short walk down a hallway and go unnoticed. His biggest fear was that once his classmates learned he had Tourette, or observed him ticcing, they would mock and even ostracize him.

It was a legitimate fear. In TV shows popular with adolescents and teenagers, Tourette tends to be portrayed as all about cursing—all *shit-talk*. One show seemed to be particularly well known among kids Michael's age, a 2007 episode of *South Park* titled "Le Petit Tourette."

100

In it, a character named Cartman pretends he has Tourette syndrome so he can get away with swearing whenever he pleases.

The Hollywood version of Tourette rarely gets it right and may have even cemented the stigma. There was one instance that stands out, though. After *The Simpsons* aired a segment in which Bart mimicked the symptoms of Tourette in 1993, a teenager with Tourette from Seattle emailed the show's creators and complained. They removed the segment from the show.

When I talked with Tourette Association CEO Amanda Talty, she agreed that the news media tends to cover only sensationalized cases of Tourette. "It's very challenging to get media attention unless the tics are particularly egregious or someone they deem notable has it. In other words, anything sensational or over the top," she said.

In one Canadian study that reviewed fictional films and TV shows between 1976 and 2010, researchers found that many of the shows misrepresented Tourette syndrome, portraying those with the condition as eccentric or involved in negative family, school, and social dynamics: Of the characters imitating Tourette, nearly three-quarters exhibited coprolalia, giving "the misleading impression that coprolalia is the most common symptom" of Tourette syndrome, when in fact, only about 10% of people with Tourette have it.

The biggest news story involving Tourette occurred in 2018, when Grammy Award winner Billie Eilish went public with her childhood diagnosis of Tourette. When that happened, I hoped her reveal might rob the condition of some of its stigma. Nowadays, there are more and more adults with Tourette using their platforms to educate people, like David Begnaud, the lead national correspondent for *CBS Mornings*, and social media superstars and influencers like a police officer known as "Tourette's cop."

To deal with any stigma Michael might face, I tried to come up with a response he could use for whatever conceivable situation he might face in his 200-foot walk from the school's front door to the cafeteria or, later, in the classroom.

"If you feel the urge to tic, you can just raise your hand and ask to go to the bathroom, then head to the guidance office," I reminded him. I also had suggestions for how to handle bullies. "If someone bullies you, ignore them, pretend you don't hear them," I said. "But if they do it again, whisper, 'F— you.'"

I thought he would laugh at my joke. But he just looked at me as if I had told him to steal candy from the grocery store.

"I'm not gonna do that."

"Look, you can just say, 'It was my Tourette.'" I smiled.

He later told me that he hated it when I would try to coach him about how to act around his classmates. Looking back, I admit that my never-ending barrage of suggestions may have been overkill. And maybe a sign that I still had not accepted his diagnosis.

Even though a 504 Plan was not yet in place, Russ and I agreed to try to send him back to school before Michael could change his mind. I knew we needed to act during this sudden small window when Michael was willing—a window that could quickly close if something went wrong.

And I couldn't stop thinking about all the things that could go wrong.

What if he called a teacher a bitch? What if he said the "C" word? Or the N-word? *What if, what if, what if?*

But we had kept Michael out long enough, and so a full three months after his last full day in school, he and his new tutor, Richelle, met in a room off the cafeteria after school let out. One by one, the teachers came in to say hi (another one of Fayne Molloy's brilliant ideas). Michael stayed only an hour, but I felt as if weeks had passed when I picked him up.

"How did it go?"

"OK."

"Did you see anyone you knew?"

"Yes, my teachers came in to say hi."

"Did you run into any kids?"

"Nobody I knew."

It was anticlimactic—a good thing, in my opinion.

The language arts teacher, who had been one of Michael's favorites, lingered and chatted with Michael. She told him he had the choice to either read the play *A Midsummer Night's Dream*, then write an extensive report, or come back to school and act in the play with his classmates.

Right then and there, he chose to perform in the play. Apparently, reading Shakespeare and writing a report on it was so dreadful that he decided to face his biggest fear: 200 sixth graders.

It seemed like a shocking choice at the time, but like singing or playing music, acting, as we would learn, was another focused activity that put Michael in the no-ticcing zone.

The following Monday, May 2, Michael went back to school and attended English class because they were holding auditions for the play. He also went to phys ed. The Geodon was not a cure-all, but Michael's tics were more subdued, and so far, there were no apparent side effects.

It was incredibly, remarkably uneventful and anticlimactic. For him.

But to me, it was clear we had turned a corner. It reminded me of his first day of kindergarten, when I was as nervous as he was.

That night, he seemed fine, if not happy.

But we didn't want to rush things; the plan was to continue doing the homebound tutoring program until he started back full-time in a few weeks. It felt like the safety net he needed.

The next week he followed the original game plan, going in for a few hours each day. Even that little break gave me some much-needed breathing space. I had a lot to get caught up on. There were papers to grade and then final exams for the class I taught, which was ending on May 5. In the end, I found my groove and even came to enjoy teaching, or at least parts of it.

I was also the co-chair of Author's Day, an event at Katie's elementary school. We had arranged for a children's book author and illustrator who was open about the fact that she had learning disabilities to come lecture and do a book signing. I planned to bring Michael along to the event.

I had heard Patricia Polacco speak several years earlier, before Michael had been diagnosed, and she made a big impression. A magnificent storyteller who dressed in bright colors and wore her hair in a tight bun atop her head, she expounded on what it was like for kids with learning differences, and she dared them to dream. "Don't you let anybody talk you out of yourself," she said. "You can rise and rise and rise."

Polacco talked to the kids about her dyslexia, dysgraphia, and a few other learning disabilities that hadn't prevented her from writing 77 books. "When I was little, they didn't know what to do with people like me," she recalled. "I couldn't read or do math until I was 14." Every day, she said, she went home crying because kids teased her.

"But I rose above it," she said. "I worked around it and used it to make my life something extraordinary. And that's how I want you to think about it."

One of Polacco's books, *The Junkyard Wonders,* about her group of misfit friends and a life-changing teacher in a special education classroom, was based on her childhood experiences.

My friend and co-chair of Author's Day had given Michael a copy because there happened to be a kid in the "junkyard" who had Tourette, along with a girl who had diabetes and one who didn't speak. There are heartbreaking scenes, including one in which a girl is not allowed to sit at a table with a friend because she's in the "junkyard."

Toward the end of the book, the teacher takes the class to a junk-yard and asks them to "collect everything that could be made into something new." Together, they use their finds to build a model airplane, nicknamed "the Junkyard Wonder."

That's what I wanted to do: gather information and arm myself and my son with all sorts of stuff that could rebuild him into something better—a version of himself that would be sturdy and strong but also had wings. Because at the time, I still felt as though Michael was cursed. Instead of accepting his diagnosis, I was still hell-bent on finding an antidote.

"Don't you see what a junkyard is?" the teacher in the book asked. "Oh, it is a place of wondrous possibilities! What some see as bent and broken throwaways are amazing things waiting to be made into something new. Something unexpected. Something surprising."

I still smile every time I read those lines. How I wanted Michael to see himself like that—a wonder just waiting to be transformed into something new.

The evening after the event, James Durbin, a young man who had come to accept his condition, was eliminated from *American Idol*.

Later that week, I went to school for a meeting with Michael's guidance counselor and the school psychologist to draft his 504 Plan. The date happened to be 25 years to the day that Russ and I had graduated from college. I put the picture of the two of us in cap and gown, windblown and wrinkle-free, on the bookshelf in our new bedroom. We looked young and unaware of what the future might bring. I could not have imagined the arguments and angst, the bedtime prayers and tear-stained pillows.

I went alone to the meeting, but I was heavily armed. I had done my research and had written in my trusty notebook a list of requests I wanted to be included in Michael's 504 Plan, after being schooled by both Molloy and Tony Mullen, who had been named National Teacher of the Year in 2009 and whom I had interviewed for a project. He had given me some insights into the way special education works—or, in many cases, does not work—before I had a child of my own with challenges.

The first thing I asked for was an "escape plan" in writing, so Michael could leave the room if he needed to, plus weekly updates from his teachers, until he transitioned back to school full-time. I also asked for a reduced homework load, extra time on tests, and a separate place to take tests, as needed. I also wanted something in writing to hand to substitute teachers so that if Michael started ticcing or needed to leave the classroom, they would know why.

The guidance counselor and psychologist were nice—chummy, even—until I asked about an IEP. Brushing aside my concerns that a 504 Plan wouldn't be enough, they both agreed that Michael did not need an IEP because his grades were good; the fact that he was in some advanced classes, including Spanish and honors English, was apparently another strike against him. The dirty little secret of special education is that most kids have to be failing, not just struggling, to access services.

It seemed as though they had discussed this in advance, putting the kibosh on it in unison, as if they were on autopilot.

I was disappointed but not surprised.

As Walisever, who serves on the TAA's education committee, later explained, "You are working with a team of people at school who may be well meaning, but who may not be aware of the nuances of the law, and they are certainly not aware of the nuances of Tourette syndrome and of the fact that a student with Tourette, OCD, anxiety, and poor handwriting can still be a straight-A student while having other functional, behavioral, and emotional issues," she said.

Since the 504 usually does not cost the school district any money, schools typically tend to be more generous with it, she added. However, an IEP requires specialized personnel and services such as occupational therapy, a resource room, and speech and language therapy, all of which cost the school money. "That's why parents have to fight harder to move from the 504 to the IEP," she said.

"The school is legally not required to provide the student the Cadillac, or the best, education. It's just the Honda, the good enough, so they can access what their peers access," explained Walisever. "It's also not about helping the student live up to their potential."

In other words, the school was not obligated to help Michael excel, or to maximize his potential; they only needed to even the playing field enough for him to just get by.

Getting by was not what we wanted for our son. Or our daughter. That, Russ and I agreed on.

I wanted to believe the two nice women who assured me that the 504 Plan would be sufficient. They seemed very capable, if not amenable, but I had a feeling that things might go south pretty quickly, that we would be hearing *Sorry, we'd like to help you, but we can't* again in our future.

For the moment, though, I played nice. Michael was finally back in school full-time, after all. Between that and the tutor, we were all hoping to just make it through to the end of the school year, which was only a month away, with Michael getting decent grades and not having to repeat the year. I told myself I would figure out how to get him an IEP when school started come fall.

A week later, I was notified in writing by the head of the Board of Education that Michael's homebound tutor was being terminated. I hadn't realized that once Michael was back in school, he would no longer be eligible for this service.

Both of his tutors had been a lifeline, and I hoped we could continue with Richelle to make sure Michael was able to keep up with what was going on in the classroom, which would be more stressful and demanding than learning in our living room. Now, I worried that between being home for three months, going back to school in person, and losing his tutor, it would be like going from Pee Wee football to the NFL.

I emailed Michael's guidance counselor to share my concerns, aware that I needed to build some evidence for the battle I might have to wage for Michael's IEP the following fall; I thought it was important to put everything in writing if the shit hit the fan, as I suspected it might without an IEP. I hoped this virtual paper trail would serve me well later.

I pointed out that the nature of Tourette is that tics tend to wax and wane, and while we hoped he would continue to improve, he might very well end up missing more school. The email I received back was clear: "I completely understand the situation; unfortunately, I don't have control of how the program works."

Michael didn't seem to mind, so I tried to take it in stride, given that there were only three weeks of school left. *He just needs to make it out of sixth grade,* I told myself.

On the bright side, on May 26, Michael performed his part in *A Midsummer's Night Dream* without ticcing. His social life was also improving. He went to a local carnival with a girl he liked and agreed to let us throw a party for some of his sixth-grade friends over Memorial Day weekend. While the kids swam and ran around the backyard, we barbecued, the music playing on our speakers drowning out any of Michael's tics. It felt as if life were getting back to normal.

Chapter 12

Looking for the Cracks

The summer of 2011 was a quiet one, literally and figuratively. Without the stress or pressures of school, and with the possible benefits of Geodon, Michael's ticcing was way down.

Katie went off to camp in Vermont, a place she loved, and Russ, Michael, and I took a trip to Maine to visit Russ's cousin Frank, who worked in the music industry. He invited a client over for dinner who had worked with grieving kids, helping them use songwriting as art and a way to express themselves. Russ, Frank, and I sat in the dining room, drinking wine and eavesdropping on Billy and Michael chatting and strumming on guitars, as Billy helped Michael write his own song. It was one of several things we did over the summer to encourage Michael's musical talents and build his confidence. Michael's interest in music had increased, and he continued playing over the summer. By now, I realized that music might actually help heal him or at least get him through middle and high school.

Still, July wasn't even over before I began to stress about what the fall would bring. I worried that without an IEP, returning to the middle school for seventh grade would be like rescuing a wounded dolphin, nursing it back to health, then throwing it into a shark tank.

I decided to toughen Michael up a bit in case he was bullied. At the very least, I wanted to help him care less what people thought of him. That's difficult at age 12—or any age.

After reading a few child-rearing books and articles, I decided to teach him how to respond to bullies without resorting to violence.

One article I read on various ways to disarm a bully, advised kids to remain calm and unemotional, exude confidence, and not allow a bully to get under their skin.

I had the idea of coming up with clever retorts he could use on demand. Sitting in our backyard, I told Michael, "I want you to call me names, and make fun of me, and I'll give some responses to show different ways you can deal with it."

He paused for a few seconds, then grinned.

"You have a big nose."

"My olfactory skills are heightened. And I can sniff out jerks like you pretty easily."

"Your hair is red and brown. And you're chubby."

Wow. This kid could sling insults like my brothers.

"You're old."

"Older and wiser," I said, and then we both began to laugh.

By the time school started on September 1, I felt I had done everything I could to set Michael up for success: I had attended a local Tourette conference and special education meetings and picked the brains of everyone I met. I also found a nearby therapist who was trained in CBIT (though Michael was unenthusiastic and lost interest before they could get very far). On my own, I also secretly began researching private schools. I needed a Plan B in case all the pieces didn't fall into place and Michael couldn't thrive in the public school system.

I also made an appointment with an education advocate to figure out what the next steps were to get Michael the elusive IEP. She explained it would be a tough sell because he was doing well academically. Despite missing three months of school, his end-of-year report card listed A's and B's. She said that as long as we could keep Michael in school by decreasing his stress and ticcing, she didn't think we needed to consider special education services, but if he ended up missing a significant amount of school again, we could revisit this. She suggested we forgo the PPT meeting, which stands for Planning and Placement Team, to discuss a possible IEP, and instead beef up his 504 Plan a bit.

It was discouraging and surprising that even if an advocate walked us through the steps, it was a long shot.

Finally, a couple of weeks before school started, I emailed Michael's guidance counselor to make sure our son would be on her radar. When I didn't hear from her, I followed up with a phone call to see whether she'd had a chance to review the 504 Plan. "I have a stack of 504 Plans on my desk," she said.

~

Though Michael's ticcing had eased over the summer, on the first day of seventh grade, I heard him making sounds again. Rather than outright cursing, by now, Michael could (mostly) stifle the tics to the extent that it sounded as if he were mumbling under his breath. During the first week of school, he managed to hold them in all day, then blurted them out all at once when he arrived home.

It was clear, though, that he was uncomfortable at school. "I hardly know any of the kids," he complained. He'd get especially upset when kids would say, "Stop saying 'shit!'" or if someone asked, "Why are you making that sound?" And kids asked this question all the time.

"They must be thinking, *What's wrong with that kid?*" he said one night.

"There are lots of kids who are different in middle school," I said.

He just looked at me and said, "They're all perfect." This was a sentiment he would repeat over and over that fall.

I couldn't convince him to use the comments as an opportunity to explain his Tourette. To him, that would be akin to admitting he was a freak.

Years later, he told me that he felt completely alone. No one understood what he was going through, but he also didn't want to tell anyone what he was going through. "It was a vicious cycle," he told me.

"You felt that even I didn't understand?"

"Yes."

He was right. I would never know what it felt like to have no control over the sounds or words coming out of your own mouth. One morning, when I tried to rouse Michael for school, the first thing he said was, "You have no idea the pain I feel."

I had a sense of what it was like to not fit in. I was a painfully shy child through elementary school, too embarrassed to raise my hand in class.

My second-grade teacher called my mother in for a conference half-way through the year. "She told me she thought you were retarded—that's the word she used," my mother told me time and again.

My mother was no squeaky wheel, but she lashed out at the teacher.

"She gets straight A's!" she yelled. "How can she be retarded?"

Looking back, it's absurd that the teacher mistook my being shy for having a learning disability and, even worse, that she used the word *retarded* to describe a student.

That insecurity stayed with me for 30 years, until I read the best-selling book *Quiet*, by Susan Cain. The author described me perfectly when she wrote: "[Introverts] listen more than they talk, think before they speak, and often feel as if they express themselves better in writing than in conversation. They tend to dislike conflict. Many have a horror of small talk but enjoy deep discussions."

Things got worse for me in sixth grade, the year Michael had just completed, the worst year of his life. Mine too.

That's when my best friend began to ignore me, holding court on the playground with girls hanging on her every word as I stood alone, wondering how I would get through two 20-minute recesses a day. It was like being alone at a wedding where everyone else knew each other—and, worse yet, had brought dates.

Of course, middle school is miserable for many of us, and I knew that Michael would eventually get through it, as I had. For me, everything changed in seventh grade when a new batch of students transferred into my school, and I made new friends—many of whom I kept throughout high school. If you asked my high school classmates, they would be shocked to hear that I ever felt as if I didn't fit in; by the time I graduated, I had plenty of close friends.

I told Michael that story, hoping he, too, would soon have a similar turning point.

"What does that have to do with me?" he asked. He had a point: My experience, while painful, was nothing compared to what he was going through.

Most of the time he refused to talk about what was going on at school. But without fail, he would open up at bedtime when he was supposed to be asleep, or in the morning, when he was supposed to be getting ready for school, and I was still in a pre-coffee stupor. I learned to grab my mug of coffee and bring it upstairs with me, because I couldn't tackle our early-morning conversations without the jolt of caffeine and the scent of Trader Joe's pumpkin spice coffee.

"Mom, nobody likes me. They all hate me."

Michael had just woken up and was still in bed, the shades still drawn, the blue walls still dark. It was only 6:45 and I had already made Katie lunch, cleaned the breakfast dishes, emptied the dishwasher, and thrown in a load of laundry. His words stopped me in my tracks.

Michael was in the fetal position, a small, boy-size lump beneath his blue patchwork quilt. All I could see was a mound of thick brown hair the color of milk chocolate, and his profile. To my eyes, he still had the same baby face he did at 2, his long eyelashes the first thing people noticed about his face.

"At lunch, if there are too many kids at a table, they vote on who has to leave. It's always me."

"When was the last time this happened?" I asked.

"Yesterday. Someone said, 'Who votes that Michael leaves?' They all raised their hands."

I knew he didn't have many friends, but I hadn't realized he was a target. It was heartbreaking.

He continued to describe other incidents.

"Another day, I went to buy a bottle of water and someone put my lunch on another table."

"How long has this been going on?"

"Weeks."

I wanted to wrap my arms around my baby and make it all better like I had when he was young. I remembered how easily consoled he was as an infant, and thought, *Why is it so hard now?*

I sat down on his bed and rubbed his back, deciding to let him sleep through the first period. When I came back and tried to wake him a half-hour later, he said, "I'm scared."

"Scared of what?"

"I'm terrified of school," he said. I would later learn that what Michael was expressing is actually a medical condition called school avoidance disorder. I have two good friends whose children experienced this problem recently.

Meanwhile, our morning and evening rituals continued, with Michael venting and sometimes crying, repeating the same lines again and again: "I hate school" and "I'm miserable."

"What specifically do you hate?" I asked one day.

He rattled off a list.

"Grades. Kids. Teachers. Tests. Homework."

Given Michael's angst, my own inner dialogue was never-ending, like having the same bad dream every night. *What if he turns to drugs or booze to placate himself? What if he becomes so depressed he harms himself? What if he hates himself forever?* And always, *What else can I do to fix this?*

I emailed his teachers and set up an appointment with the therapist who had treated him the previous spring to get some advice. Michael had always had difficulty making friends, but he had never been targeted or been an outcast before. Then again, that was before the Tourette diagnosis.

Next, I emailed the principal and asked her if she wouldn't mind sitting down with Michael to chat. They had developed a nice rapport after he took the CMTs in her office, and I thought she might help us figure out how to make his life less miserable at school.

It was a bold move for me. Normally, I might ask a teacher or the guidance counselor to weigh in, but I was not a mom who called the principal to ask for a meeting. Until now.

We met the next day in her office. She was tall, thin, and athletic-looking, with short, sandy-blonde hair. As we sat in her office, Michael spoke freely. He said he didn't like being on Team One (referring to the two-team structure of his seventh-grade class). He told her his friends were on Team Two (I wasn't sure which friends he was referring to), and she quickly said he could switch teams if he liked.

"How long would it take?" he asked.

"Two minutes," she said.

Michael smiled.

Then the principal suggested that Michael do a PowerPoint presentation about Tourette to his classmates. Surprisingly, he was game. I am not sure why he was so open to these suggestions, but perhaps it was because the principal had suggested it, and he had come to trust her, as I had. On our way out of her office, she put her hand on Michael's shoulder and said, "That's the best thing about being the boss—you get to do things like this." I wanted to hug her.

That night, when I told Russ about our meeting with Shelley, I said, "She's a rock star."

Two days of unbridled optimism and excitement passed. My hope was that Michael could remain in the public school system for the next six years, instead of transferring to a private school, as Russ and I had been discussing—or, rather, arguing about, since Russ was adamant that we couldn't afford it. I desperately hoped the PowerPoint would make a difference, and that the kids would accept him. I hoped the fighting with Russ would finally end.

~

Then, two days after our meeting, I received a mass email from the Board of Education explaining that our rock star principal was taking a leave of absence pending an investigation into an incident that happened when she ran a day care center 17 years ago.

A five-minute Google search revealed that a preschooler had been left in a van during a field trip to a museum under the principal's watch; an investigation later cleared her. My concern, of course, was that Michael's best advocate might be leaving the school. I felt as if the best date of my life had turned out to be married.

I decided that this would be a sign: If the principal stayed in the school, we would stay. If she got fired, we would transfer Michael to a private school. The fact that he was starting to make friends, but also seemed agitated and was ticcing a lot, added to my inner turmoil. Every time I heard another story of a kid being bullied or teased at the school, I panicked, thinking, *What if they do something to Michael?* I just wanted kids to be kind to him.

Introverts like me tend to have anxiety about making the wrong decisions, about matters large and small. When it comes to shopping, I don't buy; I browse. In a restaurant, I am the last person at the table to place an order. And I am a champion procrastinator. In 1997 I bought a book called *It's About Time! The 6 Styles of Procrastination and How to Overcome Them.* I have never cracked it open.

And so, I went back and forth about whether Michael should go to private school, never mind the fact that Russ wasn't on board. The principal incident added a sense of urgency to what had until then been a fact-finding mission to learn about private schools.

It seemed to me that private school would be our son's best chance to assimilate, because the environment and people would presumably be more compassionate and accommodating, even though most do not offer official accommodations (other than schools for kids with learning differences which would not be a good fit because his disability was not severe enough).

At the public school, I worried that Michael was an easy target. Students with disabilities are two to three times more likely to be bullied than typical students, according to Pacer's National Bullying Prevention Center. Research has shown that kids with Tourette syndrome are also more likely to experience bullying as well as a fair amount of teasing, taunts, and rejection from their peers. According to the most recent TAA impact survey, 70% of kids with Tourette said they have been bullied as a result of their condition.

Sometimes the jabs are subtle. One woman I spoke with who had multiple motor tics throughout middle school and high school, including a nose twitch, confessed the tic had earned her the nickname "Bunny."

I have read many stories from all over the country about people with Tourette who have been mistreated, or even suspended from school. There have also been several reports of high school students being banned from sports for making disruptive sounds. An Indiana college student was kicked off of campus because he had Tourette. A 15-year-old ticcing teenager was asked to leave a movie theater in Oklahoma (she later became a TAA Youth Ambassador). And many people have been fired from their jobs because of Tourette, even though this violates the Americans with Disabilities Act.

It did bother me, however, that the private schools in the area seemed like bastions of privilege. At one school I toured, every child had their own Apple computer. As I walked around, the plush, carpeted halls and half-empty classrooms exuded the calm and quiet of a resort hotel. At another school, the grounds abutted a famous film director's home.

But there was one school I liked, an odd-shaped structure built in the 1960s and even a bit run-down, though every bit as expensive as the others.

Inside, the walls were Barney-the-dinosaur purple, and the director of admissions explained that students called teachers by their first names. The student-to-teacher ratio was also a plus: There were only about five to seven kids in each math class. The school also had a teen center for the seventh and eighth graders—a room with a giant plaid piece of furniture two stories high, part couch, part bunk bed, with a Partridge Family vibe. There was also a music room with a piano, a dozen electric guitars, and a nice drum set.

"Oh, my," Michael said with a grin as he peered inside. By now, he was all about music; we had recently enrolled him in School of Rock, a performance-based program that combined music lessons with weekly group rehearsals.

Most people know the movie *School of Rock* and the spin-off musical comedy on Broadway. The origins of the program Michael was now in are a bit fuzzy, but from what I gathered online, the original School of Rock was launched in Philadelphia in 1998. The franchise now counts nearly 60,000 students at 300 locations throughout the U.S. and in several other countries.

Instead of teaching kids to read music, School of Rock uses a technique called song-based learning. The whole idea is to prepare students to perform live in real venues. One of their taglines is "Where music students grow into real musicians." There are three performance seasons a year, and for each, kids choose a different band or artist, then learn and play their music, working alone with an instructor once a week. They also meet with their bandmates weekly to practice.

The first time I visited, I whispered to the clean-cut, cheerful guy behind the desk (who turned out to be Steve Kennedy, the owner) that Michael had Tourette. I told him I was nervous about what the other kids would think.

Steve told me not to worry, that School of Rock was a welcoming place.

I asked if I could look around. There were small practice rooms, each with a tiny internal window; a lounge papered with rock posters and graffiti; and more rock posters everywhere. In the upstairs practice room there were five kids, maybe 7 to 17 years old, playing drums, guitar, and singing...and I could not believe how good they sounded. Even with Tourette, I had a hunch that Michael might fit in here.

When I returned with Michael the next week, we met Byl Cote, the music director, who, with his long black hair and gruff manner, was "kind of a scary-looking dude," as Michael whispered to me. He turned out to be a taskmaster who was so passionate and energetic that the kids couldn't help but be inspired.

Soon after his first lesson, Michael chose to do the Black Sabbath show, which was by invitation only and required extra practice sessions. I would have preferred the Rolling Stones, but Michael seemed willing to do the work, so I gladly resigned myself to listening to Ozzy Osbourne for the next few months.

Michael was also invited to play guitar in what was known as the house band. I already knew my son had a lovely voice, but it came as a surprise that he had any real musical talent.

"It's our advanced group," Byl told me. "They practice once a week, and they play gigs at local bars and events."

"He's only 12!" I said, with a quizzical look, thinking that I did not want my kid *playing gigs in bars*.

Byl grinned. "The drummer's 8—you should hear him."

I was sold on SOR, as groupies called it—and Michael was sold on the private school with the cool music room. But it came with a steep price tag like all the others: $34,000 a year. In the eight months since Michael had been diagnosed with Tourette, I'd been draining our bank account with all the health care visits not covered by insurance, adding to our debt.

Yet I had seen Russ come up with money for things before, like his boat. He defended that purchase—and still does—as his only form of relaxation, pointing out that it was a 21-foot used Boston Whaler he shared with a friend who split the costs. I told myself we could make private school work somehow, even if we had to take out a loan.

I decided to broach the subject with my husband over a cocktail. I knew I had to make Russ feel as if the decision to send Michael to private school were his. I imagined joking about it someday, as we did over other disputes where I'd gotten my way, that it had all been Russ's idea to send Michael to private school. That is, if there was a someday. Given the level of tension between Russ and me, I wasn't always so sure.

Things didn't go quite as I had planned. After Michael and I had visited the school for a second time, I went for a run before dinner and Russ came along. But by the time we got to the park near our house, I'd begun to cry.

"I'm leaning towards transferring him," I said, almost in a whisper.

"He just had a great weekend with his school friends. Maybe this is the start of a new phase," Russ said.

"I just don't think they can give him what he needs to feel comfortable in his own skin," I said. "If he stays there, he could end up...lost."

We stood stock-still now, on the path descending into the park.

"He won't get lost with us as his parents," Russ said.

"That's not true! He could get in with the wrong crowd. And he's never met his potential in the public school system!" My voice was getting louder, and I was way off script, almost out of control, but I couldn't stop myself. "I'm on the brink of a nervous breakdown!" I shouted. "I don't know how much more I can take."

Russ was red in the face too. "Do you want us to go bankrupt?" he shouted back. "We *can't afford it!*" he snapped, his nostrils flaring in a way that let me know he was really angry.

"What are we supposed to do, let him fail? If he continues to lollygag, he'll be in remedial classes by the time he's in high school."

Then, without thinking about it, I hissed, "Private school will cost you a lot less than alimony for life."

I had not planned to threaten divorce, but once I did, I was surprised by how good it felt to put it all on the line.

I think I surprised Russ too.

~

Exactly two weeks after the public school principal was put on leave, the Board of Education reinstated her. The decision made me pull back from my full-throttle private school campaign, much to Russ's relief. Michael was in school full-time. He had friends. He was still ticcing, but he was functioning. *Maybe it will work out after all.*

Then in October, without any notice, Michael was taken out of Spanish A (the advanced class) and moved into the B class. Spanish was one of the few classes he actually liked, so this was a red flag for me. I started checking in with a few of his teachers to see how he was performing, and the response from his science teacher caught me off guard. "Michael is giving a presentation on volcanoes with his independent research group on Friday. I am concerned because his work is not at the same level as the three other students in his group. I have tried to encourage him to work on the project at home, but so far he has not."

I emailed back that he'd get the work done over the weekend, and the two of us worked for hours researching volcanoes for his presentation. It seemed as though he might have done some research on his own, but definitely not six weeks' worth. I hadn't pitched in with his work for a long, long time, but I told myself it was no big deal.

The next week the teacher emailed me again to say that Michael had created eight slides for his volcano project, but now they were missing. He needed to recreate eight slides by the next day.

I read the email around 2 p.m. on a Monday, just as school was ending. I called her, and she picked up.

"I can't imagine how this happened," she began. "The media center said the slides were saved to a website, but they must have been deleted."

I made a note of how she didn't directly blame Michael for deleting the slides.

"I'm afraid he still has to present it to the class on Friday."

That meant he had four days to do a project three other students had been working on all semester and one day to complete half of the semester's work. "I passed him against my better judgment," she continued, referring to his midterm grade, which had been a B. "If he were my son, though, I'd think he was playing me."

I didn't admit this to the teacher, but I also suspected he was lying about creating the slides in the first place. At the same time, I thought the teacher should have been more on top of what her students were doing. But maybe I should have been as well.

"How is he in class?" I asked.

"He just zones out in front of the computer," she said. "He was looking at pictures of earthquakes, not volcanos."

I remember sitting at my own computer, holding the phone in my hand and thinking, *This can't be possible. Has he really done no work in science after two and a half months of school?* I began to type—tapping the keyboard quietly—to make sure I captured the conversation verbatim.

"Given that he missed three months of school last year, my husband and I are less concerned about what his grades are at this point," I said. "I want to make sure he's learning."

I will never forget what she said next: "Well, he's not."

At that moment, I realized I had made a huge mistake: I had put too much faith in a system that had failed him. It made me wonder what the hell was going on in Michael's other classes.

I had been concerned that I had been acting like an annoying, overprotective, pushy mother. But as I sat there, the adrenaline rushing through my veins, I thought, *This is my son. Something terrible has happened to him. He has Tourette. Does anybody give a flying fuck?*

I decided then and there that I had to become an alpha mom, one who would never again be caught behind the eight ball.

We spoke for a few more minutes and came up with a compromise: Michael would get a three-day extension, and again, I promised I would help get him back on track.

"He's better than this," the teacher said. "I know what he's capable of."

So did I.

I hung up the phone and thought of all the emails I had sent to the guidance counselor and teachers, hoping to prevent this. I thought I could protect him from falling through the cracks. I'd forgotten that my child is the type who looks for the cracks.

When I asked Michael what had happened, he had no answers or excuses, which made me suspect that, indeed, he had heard the words *independent study* and decided he didn't need to do any of the work. I blamed myself. Clearly, I shouldn't have let him do an independent project for 10 weeks without checking in with him periodically. At the time, I was still in the classic Italian-mother-whose-son-who-could-do-no-wrong mode.

But in the end, I realized that the science teacher did me a huge favor.

If she hadn't been so honest, I never would have known that my son was barely getting by in school.

Chapter 13

In Vino Veritas

The next day, I set up a team meeting with Michael's teachers. I wanted to get a handle on how he was doing in other classes, find out whether he was ticcing, and beef up his 504 Plan. We were allotted 40 minutes.

I was happy that Russ was planning to attend, even though this was mostly a fact-finding mission, and most likely nothing would be decided or resolved.

I shoved a piece of Halloween candy into my mouth in the car.

The meeting was held in the principal's office, and every teacher was there except one (I was told they are required by law to attend such meetings), plus the principal, the school psychologist, and the guidance counselor. All of us squeezed around the same table where Michael had taken the CMTs eight months earlier. One by one, Michael's teachers offered a brief progress report; the news was not good.

"He sits there and daydreams a lot," one teacher said.

The others nodded in agreement.

Michael was struggling the most in math, partly because it was during the first period and he was having difficulty getting up, probably because Geodon made him groggy.

"Can we switch him to a later class?" the principal asked. I always felt she had Michael's back.

"I already have 27 kids in that class," said the math teacher. "Michael would make it 28."

"How many are in Michael's class now?" I asked.

"Twenty-seven. I think a better solution would be to move him to the B math class."

I wasn't quick enough to respond to the math teacher. But this time, I didn't have to be. Russ was with me, and he thinks on his feet, a good trait in a person who has to make split-second life-and-death decisions for work. And unlike me, he doesn't get tongue-tied when challenged.

"This is a kid who was one of three students placed into the advanced math program in second grade," he began. It was the moment I had been waiting for. My husband coming through for me. For Michael.

"He can do the work," he said.

"He can't keep up," the math teacher said. "I have 26 other kids in the class."

Russ remained calm and continued talking.

"Have you seen his CMT scores?" he asked. "Even last year, right after he was just diagnosed with Tourette, they were high. He's capable of doing the work; he's just going through a difficult time."

The teacher didn't back down. Neither did Russ.

But he remained poised, even-tempered, humble, diplomatic.

"He's two classes behind right now," the math teacher said. "He'll never be able to catch up before the marking period is over."

I finally spoke, offering the same spiel I gave the science teacher the week before.

"I am not concerned about grades. What we're concerned about is that he's learning. We already hired a tutor. Fortunately, the home-bound tutor agreed to stay on, and my husband is helping Michael with homework on the other nights. I am sure we can get him back up to speed."

"He's two classes behind," she repeated. "And he failed the last quiz."

"We've been working on the division problems," Russ said. "I took a lot of math classes, and I think he's getting it."

The back-and-forth continued for a while until the principal suggested we try a pass/fail system for the marking period.

The bar had been lowered a lot, but it seemed like a good compromise.

A few other things we agreed on: I would send an email to Michael's teachers on Monday evening asking what tests, quizzes, and projects were planned for the week, and they would respond via email. The teachers would also begin collecting data on off-task behavior like daydreaming, requests to leave class, and ticcing. Our math tutor would also speak with Michael's math teacher to make a schedule of catch-up work and tests. Finally, we would work with the principal to arrange for a presentation to the staff on Tourette and, possibly, Michael's PowerPoint presentation, and we'd beef up the 504 Plan to incorporate some of the new accommodations.

On the walk back to the car, I turned to Russ, who seemed like the real rock star.

"You were *awesome*. Thank you."

Then we talked about the mind-numbing revelation that Michael had not been doing much work in *any* classes so far, not just science. Why had no one noticed? Why had no one told us?

Tony Mullen, the National Teacher of the Year I had interviewed the year before, had said something that stayed with me. "The best teachers know that each and every child arrives at their classroom door with a unique and intriguing, yet incomplete, story.... The really good teachers are able to read a child's story and recognize the remarkable opportunity to help author that story. They know how to script confidence and success onto the blank pages. They know how to edit the mistakes. And they want to help write a happy ending."

If there was going to be a happy ending to this story, I knew I had to write it myself.

I thought back to all of the parents I knew who related how teachers had told them to lower their expectations. And I thought, *Why should I lower my expectations? It may be your job to educate the masses, but it's my job to maximize my kid's potential. Now please get the hell out of my way.*

Russ was as riled up as I was. We had two months until the end of the semester. Two months to get Michael back on track. We divvied up the subjects: Russ would take math (with the tutor's help), science, and Spanish. I would take care of English and history. We were on the same page and working on this together. Finally.

I felt a huge amount of guilt for not catching on to the situation sooner, but now that I knew, I intended to reverse Michael's downward spiral. I knew this child better than anyone, and I knew he had something locked inside him. I just wanted to find the key.

It was not enough to make sure he wasn't going to fail. It was beginning to dawn on me that I was not going to settle for his languishing in the middle, either.

~

Two days after we met with Michael's teachers, we left for a vacation in California, starting in Los Angeles, then driving north to the Bay

128

Area to spend Thanksgiving with Russ's Aunt Liz and Uncle Charlie. We viewed them as the cooler, thinner, younger version of my in-laws.

In the months leading up to the trip, Aunt Liz kept insisting we leave the kids with her overnight and head to Napa Valley, and after some resistance, we accepted her offer. I was still on edge, tense, and brusque with the kids and Russ. Being alone in wine country changed that. It was here, where we spent a carefree day tasting wine, having a quiet meal, and staying in a charming inn, that we had some of our first conversations about Michael's education that didn't end in an argument.

As we meandered from winery to winery along postcard-perfect roads lined with vineyards, we talked about Michael with a clear-eyed, 3,000 miles-from-home perspective.

We agreed that Michael had never lived up to his potential.

"Will he ever, in public school?" I wondered aloud. "Even I never thought it would come to this—that he would fall so far behind that they would want to put him in less challenging classes."

"He'll be bored and act out," Russ said.

"This is a kid who failed, but the school failed him too," I added. "At the rate he's going, he will be in remedial classes by high school."

We discussed it like two adults with a dilemma. Maybe for the first time.

"If we transfer him and he loses all contact with his friends, he'll be angry, but if he stays and ends up getting bullied and fails, we'll all be distraught," I said. "I couldn't live with myself."

"And if he needs an IEP, the process would probably take six months, so we're talking about the fall of eighth grade. He'd lose a year, and it seems like a pretty crucial one. And he would hate it if he had to repeat a year."

Russ sighed. Then he brought up the cost.

"We've spent almost $15,000 out of pocket on medical bills since January," he said.

I knew I was spending carelessly, maybe even recklessly, in my quest for a cure. But this number shocked me. I had never added up the bills.

Our conversation jumped back and forth between Michael and which vineyards to visit. We decided to hit Chateau Montelena because we love the movie *Bottle Shock*, set at the vineyard, followed by Duckhorn, to taste their famed merlot.

We also talked about the private school with the cool music room, which we'd nicknamed "the hippie school." Michael had officially been accepted. Russ's anger about the team meeting with Michael's teachers had made him more open to the idea of private school.

"What if sending him to private school doesn't necessarily solve any of his problems?" Russ asked.

"I agree, but being moved down would affect his self-esteem. He could end up floundering and, as a result, loathe himself."

Maybe it was the wine, but that day, it became clear that while Russ and I both had Michael's best interests in mind, we were worried about different things. I fretted over his emotional well-being; Russ didn't want him to become a do-nothing, spoiled rich kid with no direction. But the two of us finally seemed to be moving in the same direction.

The next day, fortuitously, sealed the deal. We met an old friend of mine for coffee.

I hadn't seen Dawn in almost 15 years, not since Russ and I went on our last big trip to California, pre-kids. We were BFFs when we worked together as junior editors in the early '90s at a now-defunct Reader's Digest–owned magazine called *American Health*. We each had two children, a girl and a boy, and when we spoke, it was mostly about the challenges of parenting our boys, who seemed to have similar issues but no diagnosis.

Now, both of them did. When her son began having trouble in school, Dawn said she suspected it was dyslexia.

Her father, she told us, was diagnosed with dyslexia as an adult, and both of her brothers had dyslexia. In an IEP meeting for her

9-year-old son, the special education coordinator told her that the school "didn't recognize the diagnosis." She transferred him to a private school, even though her husband had recently been out of work. "Transferring was a life-changer," she said.

I sat there sipping my grande skim latte feeling a combination of happiness for her and envy, aware that if I had heard this story before Michael's diagnosis, I might have concluded that she was a bit of an overprotective, anxious mother like me.

Russ asked a lot of questions. I tried to listen and keep my mouth shut. This was not a planned intervention, but it was sure coming at an opportune moment.

When we returned to Aunt Liz and Uncle Charlie's house, we learned that their son had attended the same school as Dawn's son, albeit many years earlier, and they agreed that a new school might be helpful for Michael.

I didn't mind that other people were able to convince Russ of something I was not. Instead, a serendipitous meeting of old friends over coffee put an end to the fighting, it put an end to the indecision, and it put an end to the angst. The meeting, and the much-needed respite, also ushered in a period of détente.

Soon after we returned home, we tapped into some—or possibly all—of our rainy-day fund, in the form of a home line of credit we had taken out for the renovation, and sent a check to the hippie school.

~

In early January, before Michael's first day of classes at his new school, a local TAA representative gave the lecture I had been trying to arrange at his old school for six months. Every one of Michael's new teachers sat through a two-hour presentation after school. The teachers left with a real understanding of what Michael was experiencing before they even met him.

Another sign that we had made a good choice in having Michael transfer occurred the next weekend. On a Saturday night, a girl in his new class was having a 13th birthday party, and she invited Michael (I found out later that all of the students invited the entire class to parties). Needless to say, I was anxious about dropping Michael off at a party with all strangers, but when I picked him up, he said he'd had a great time, that he had danced and was welcomed by all the kids. This was reassuring, and it gave me a sense of relief.

The faculty also seemed welcoming. In the decade since my children began school, I don't ever remember hugging a teacher. I'm not sure if that says something about me or the school system, but that changed the moment Michael started at the new school. There were so many differences between the public school system and the hippie school, but the memory that stands out most in my mind, and Russ's, is the hugging—every parent-teacher conference began with a hug. "I'll never get used to that," Russ would say every time we left the building.

What kept me up at night was worrying that Michael was so uncomfortable in his skin that he wouldn't fit in at any school. That he'd never fit in anywhere in life. I worried about what he worried about. What kept Russ up at night was that he had just written a check for $20,000, and we had no guarantees that this school would be any better than the public school. We didn't have to wait long to find out.

Michael transformed, almost overnight. At first, the new school felt like landing in sparkling, technicolor Oz after the gray of Kansas. The transition was so seamless, it was astonishing—much like suddenly noticing that your child has grown two inches when he stands next to you. There was no angst, no struggles over homework, no outbursts or rage attacks.

And there was less ticcing, too, maybe because right off the bat, Michael had given the school the OK to tell everyone about his

Tourette—even though he didn't talk about it. Most reassuring was that his teachers got to know him quickly, were aware of his condition, and really seemed to care.

As for academics, there were no tests *and no grades*, but we crossed our fingers and told ourselves it was an experiment. Our son was happy. Relaxed. Mellow. And quiet.

Our family quickly settled into a new routine. After Katie got on the school bus, Michael and I drove 15 minutes to his school and back in the afternoon (eventually, we carpooled). Most of our heart-to-heart conversations took place during these car rides. Michael talked about his new friends, and music. After school, he did his homework immediately, without prodding from us. Then he went to the basement and played guitar, practicing for his first School of Rock show.

I began to feel better about his prognosis, as well as his growth as a person. He wasn't back to his old self; he was evolving into his new self.

That's why what happened next came as such a blow.

The previous fall, when he was still attending the public school, Michael and a few of his classmates had gotten into trouble. After their usual routine of walking to the deli for sandwiches, the boys had wandered onto a seemingly abandoned property and cut a hole in the canvas covering of a small boat dry-docked there. Then they climbed in and used it as a hangout a few times, doing some minor damage along the way.

When a police officer showed up at our door, Russ and I were both home and were shocked and upset. Michael less so. He answered all of the officer's questions honestly. His friends did the same. Afterward, the officer told Russ and me that the case would most likely be referred to what's known as the Juvenile Review Board (JRB), which was created to give minors in trouble with the law a second chance and deter them from committing further offenses.

While I was waiting to hear what the next steps were, I looked in my wallet and pulled out a business card. I was hoping it would be my Get Out of Jail Free card. The card read, "Tony Mullen, National Teacher of the Year." I turned it over, where Tony had scribbled his cell phone number. I dialed it, left a message, and walked into a lecture at the hippie school entitled, appropriately enough, "The Adolescent Brain."

For the next hour, a teacher who was also a psychologist discussed what happened to behavior and judgment in adolescence due to changes in the brain, explaining the role of the prefrontal cortex—the region responsible for decision-making and judgment.

While the vast majority of a child's brain is developed by the time they are 6 years old, it's not fully developed until they are 25—and it typically takes longer in men than women. The prefrontal cortex is in the front part of the brain, the part that develops last, and it influences things like emotional control, understanding consequences, and aggression.

"Middle school is the most unsafe and unsettling time in a person's life," the speaker told the group, who, I suspected, were mostly parents of adolescents. "They have difficulty making decisions and move away from family....They have a sense of indestructibility. They want to take risks but can't see the consequences. They have an inability to see beyond the moment. Their brain loves novelty and risk-taking," she continued. "Sex, drugs, alcohol, physical heights..."

I frantically took notes. The speaker wasn't telling me a lot I didn't already know and wasn't experiencing firsthand, but she made it seem as though what had just happened to Michael was normal. I didn't tell anyone about it, but I thought back to all the mischief my three siblings and I had gotten into over the years—even Russ was no saint—and felt a bit comforted since none of us ended up behind bars.

Next, the speaker explained how to stimulate the prefrontal lobe, ostensibly to prevent the risky behavior she had just described.

"Consider getting a soft pet," she said. "Adolescents need to be comforted by responsible adults or fuzzy animals." I thought of how attached both Michael and Katie had become to Bailey in the past year. Michael even wrote a poem about her in English class.

"Encourage good friendships," the speaker continued. "And give them a bit of leeway. If you leave them alone, they feel as if they can get into a teeny bit of trouble."

I had given him a little leeway and his adolescent brain had gone haywire. I had no idea what Michael and his friends were up to, despite my hovering.

I began second-guessing every parenting decision I'd agonized over. *If I had taken him out of the public school sooner, maybe this would not have happened. If I had kept closer tabs on him, maybe this wouldn't have happened.* And, *Why did I let him go off with those boys for hours unsupervised?* I was so worried about Michael's Tourette that I forgot he was also a regular teenager, primed for trouble. I let him off the hook again.

Next, she gave a slew of practical tips, including something I took to heart: If you want to have a serious discussion with your teen, and one or both of you is upset, stand or sit next to them, rather than facing them, so they don't have to look you in the eye. I nodded, thinking of all the conversations I'd had with Michael when I was driving.

She also recommended hands-on science projects and a lot of exposure to drama and music—and joining a school rock band, if possible.

At least we were doing something right, I thought with a small smile. Just then, my phone buzzed with an unfamiliar number. *It's Tony!* I thought, jumping up to take the call outside.

Before becoming a teacher, Tony had spent 20 years as a New York City police officer, studying at night for his master's degree in education. Now he worked at an alternative high school in Connecticut, and I believed he was the one person who would know exactly what to do about our most recent problem.

"They'll 'scold' him, impose community service, and try to get the families to pay the property owner for his losses," he predicted.

"When Michael turns 16, all those records will be destroyed," he reassured me. "He will not have a criminal record."

I hung up the phone feeling relieved but also anxious. I remember thinking, *How am I going to keep this kid out of trouble for four more years? What if he gets caught stealing a Snickers bar from CVS?*

Back at home, Russ and I spoke with Michael about this latest turn of events.

"Do you realize this is serious, a crime?" I asked.

"Yes."

"How many years have we talked about making good choices?"

"Is that how I taught you to act?"

"No," he said. He seemed nonchalant, which upset me.

"Please stop crying, Mom." No boy (or boy-man, as we had taken to calling him) wants to watch his mother fall apart, but I spent several evenings sobbing on our couch, Michael's hand tentatively patting my arm.

I knew it wasn't healthy for him to see me like this, but a small part of me wondered if serving up a little Catholic guilt might do him some good. It had certainly kept my siblings and me in line as kids.

At one point I remember sitting on my bed, looking at the shelves lined with dog-eared parenting books like *Raising Cain: Protecting the Emotional Life of Boys*. What good had they done? I was in a panic, trying to convince myself that Michael wasn't destined for a life of crime. For what it's worth, Russ didn't seem to view his children's mistakes as a reflection of his parenting skills, or his persona. Maybe it was because he wasn't a mother.

What really galled me was that Michael didn't seem to be taking this matter as seriously as I thought he should. Maybe we had cut him too much slack—getting him a tutor, transferring him to a low-pressure private school, pitching in to help him with homework—with just about everything.

136

The next week, the detective informed us that the matter would be handled by the JRB, and the boys would have to divvy up restitution and do community service.

Three weeks later, Russ, Michael, and I walked into the local police precinct. We were escorted into a room and seated at a table with the JRB team, including a police officer and a social worker. I had made Michael put on khaki pants and a light-blue Oxford shirt. He looked so young, and I wondered if he would tic because he was nervous. I also wondered if he was nervous enough.

Even I had to admit he had become a little spoiled, entitled, even. I remember thinking that it was now or never: I had to turn him into a kid with a heart. A kid like the ones described in all those parenting books I had read.

Russ and I were hoping this meeting would scare Michael straight, but he still looked unfazed. We agreed: He needed to learn a lesson; he needed to know there were consequences for his actions.

As the team explained, if he screwed up again, there would be no second chance. We all nodded and said we understood as they told us what was expected going forward: 30 hours of community service (he ended up doing cleanup at a local park and volunteering at a library book sale and nursing home). He also had to check in monthly, keep a journal, and write a letter of apology to the victim. As for the money he owed, we came up with a list of chores like painting our fence, weeding, and cleaning our cars. Plus, we'd grounded him for a month. Yet Michael did not look particularly sorry.

As for me, I was polite, I was respectful, and I was crushed.

At that moment, instead of feeling angry at myself, I felt angry at Michael. I had given my all to get him through a huge life crisis, and now he had messed it up.

It was a wake-up call for me. It finally dawned on me: Maybe the only person who could help Michael succeed was Michael.

Chapter 14

Sweet Child O' Mine

One word came to mind when I walked into the Lucky Break Bar and Grill: *dive*. It was located on a busy commercial street in downtown Stamford, but when I stepped inside, it reminded me of the Jersey Shore bars where I spent my college summers.

The Lucky Break was a dark, cavernous space with a rectangular bar in the front, a stage, and about a dozen pool tables lined up in the rear. As I walked toward the stage, my boots stuck to the floor. It was a Saturday at noon, and the place smelled like a combination of antiseptic and stale beer.

It had been a week since Michael had started at his new school, and we were there for his first School of Rock gig, a show devoted to Black Sabbath. He had been preparing for three months, since October, when we enrolled him in the program.

He had taken to it immediately. I'd never seen him work so hard at anything. Every day, he'd go down to our basement to practice, surrounded by posters of the Beatles, Green Day, Rush, and Kurt Cobain. He'd blare Black Sabbath, singing, playing guitar, and drumming, and then move on to other songs he was teaching himself to play on guitar and bass. His favorites were Guns N' Roses' "Sweet Child O' Mine," "Tom Sawyer" by Rush, and any song he could find that had challenging guitar riffs.

Heavy metal reverberated through the house, and within a week or so of starting at the School of Rock, Michael had learned several songs from start to finish. When I was in my office, just above the corner of the basement where he practiced, the windows shook. You'd think the neighbors would complain, but instead, they complimented Michael on his chops. I was so happy he was happy that I didn't mind the noise.

Each week, Michael spent several hours at School of Rock taking lessons and attending mandatory band practices. In between songs, the kids passed the time in what they called the "hangout room," decorated with graffiti and plastered with more rock posters. Later, Michael told me, "For an angsty little kid with a lot of energy who never felt like he fit in, it was heaven."

He also loved that the kids called the adult teachers by their first names, and that they were treated almost like friends or family. Looking back, this dynamic is what really stayed with him. To Michael, Byl Cote, the music director, was like a mother hen. "He was the most fun and loving person, but when he needed us to be serious, he would crack the whip. He was the perfect balance."

For me, Michael's very first gig is what sticks in my mind. A burly guy with a salt-and-pepper ponytail wearing cowboy boots and a tank top that revealed tattoo-covered arms played Motown hits from his sound booth while anxious tweens and teens filed in carrying their equipment. I sat with Michael at one of the high-top tables in front of the stage, sipping a soda as we waited for Katie and Russ to arrive.

"Are you nervous?" I asked.

"A little," he said as he picked at a plate of nachos.

It had been a year to the day since Michael had started ticcing, and now he was about to play guitar and sing a solo in front of a hundred people. I couldn't help but think of James Durbin.

Unlike the concert in Carnegie Hall, I wasn't concerned that Michael would swear; it was clear by now that when he sang or played an instrument, the ticcing ceased.

I had begun to think of Michael's musical talent as a gift from God, one that came to light after his Tourette. But the fact is, there is a lot of science on music's effects on the brain.

The late neurologist Oliver Sacks, author of the best-seller turned movie *Awakenings*, also wrote a book entitled *Musicophilia: Tales of Music and the Brain*. It was packed with fascinating anecdotes about people with serious, difficult-to-treat conditions such as autism, Parkinson's disease, and schizophrenia who responded to music in a way they never did to medication.

Sacks wrote: "Music can lift us out of depression or move us to tears—it is a remedy, a tonic, orange juice for the ear. But for many of my neurological patients, music is even more—it can provide access, even when no medication can, to movement, to speech, to life. For them, music is not a luxury, but a necessity."

In *Musicophilia* (which means to love or crave music), Sacks specifically refers to the therapeutic powers of drumming, which would soon become Michael's main instrument. In the book, he recounts witnessing a drum circle of Touretters led by a young man named Matt Giordano. "Music here had a double power: first to reconfigure brain activity and bring calm and focus to people who were sometimes distracted or preoccupied by incessant tic and impulses; and second, to promote musical and special bonding with others, so that what

140

began as a miscellany of isolated, often distressed or self-conscious individuals almost instantly became a cohesive group with a single aim—a veritable drum orchestra under Matt's baton."

Unlike other creatives, musicians have brains that are unique, according to Sacks, in part because they have connections and activity that other brains lack. He wrote: "Anatomists today would be hard put to identify the brain of a visual artist, a writer, or a mathematician—but they would recognize the brain of a professional musician without a moment's hesitation."

The Tourette-music connection got some airtime after Grammy Award–winning artist Billie Eilish revealed, back in 2018, that she had Tourette. "When I'm moving around, I'm not ticcing. When I'm focusing, singing, writing, I'm not ticcing," Eilish explained in an interview with David Letterman.

The latest musician to talk about his Tourette is Scottish singing sensation Lewis Capaldi, who made headlines in 2023 when he paused a concert mid-song because he was ticcing, and his fans took over singing for him.

Reading Sacks's work and witnessing how Michael took to music made me realize that the idea of music as medicine doesn't seem so far-fetched. There's also evidence that music can help people overcome a stammer and other difficulties with language, and it's often used as a speech therapy tool. On the same day Michael performed at Carnegie Hall back in February, the 83rd Academy Awards were taking place in Los Angeles. That night, the film *The King's Speech* won two Oscars, including Best Picture. British actor Colin Firth also accepted the award for Best Actor for his role in *The King's Speech*, a film about how Prince Albert overcame his severe stuttering when he ascended the throne as King George VI after his older brother abdicated the throne in 1936. With the help of a speech therapist who used unorthodox methods, including daily vocal exercises, King George VI was able to deliver wartime radio broadcasts to the United Kingdom.

In my own life, from the lullabies that soothed both kids, to the music we played in the car when they were toddlers, including a CD called *All You Need Is Love: Beatles Music for Kids* (Michael's favorite was "Ob-La-Di, Ob-La-Da"), it was clear to me that music could pacify or improve a child's mood. But the idea that focusing on something can quell tics is not limited to the arts. Professional soccer player Tim Howard, known for his dramatic saves during the 2014 World Cup in Brazil, where he played for the U.S. Men's National Team, once said, "As soon as things get serious in front of the goal, I don't have any twitches.... It's probably because at that moment, my concentration on the game is stronger than the Tourette syndrome."

Back at the Lucky Break, Michael was simply trying to survive his first show. Dressed in Russ's Woodstock T-shirt, his long bangs covering his eyes, he was an adorable tween trying to look cool. I was reminded of a quote from music critic Lester Bangs, who said, "The only true currency in this bankrupt world is what you share with someone else when you're uncool."

Looking back, Michael agreed. "Everyone was jamming to Black Sabbath and wearing long, awful hair and baggy jeans, but nobody cared. We knew we were uncool, but it was awesome because we were playing, we were musicians," he said.

But when the lights dimmed, they actually *were* cool. To my surprise, Michael and his equally young bandmates sounded like a real band. The only difference, aside from their age, was that they were all deadly serious and sober.

As Michael played Black Sabbath, his body barely moved, but his guitar sounded good and his voice sounded even better when he belted out the dark, disturbing lyrics of the first song, called "Hole in the Sky." If they'd been there, my parents would have said, "You call that music?"

The song names were not exactly tween-appropriate either.

"War Pigs."

"Children of the Grave."

"Hand of Doom."

"Fairies Wear Boots," which I later learned is about skinheads.

Still, what I felt was grateful relief. I had taken my son to a dozen different healers who poked and prodded his body and probed his psyche. But in the end, something as simple as music had increased his confidence and stifled his ticcing. In a year, he had come so far. I left the bar knowing that *this* was the outlet he needed.

I still had no idea that music would become so central to his life, to all of our lives.

As we were leaving, Russ began chatting with Steve, the owner of our local School of Rock, who mentioned that there was also an adult band. The next week, Russ signed up to sing in the David Bowie show.

Chapter 15

Wired and Tired

When I realized that Michael's spring break occurred during a different week than Katie's, I pulled my daughter out of school, and my mother and I took the kids to Disney World. I was teaching again this semester, so we only went for a long weekend. Russ stayed home. "Once was enough," he said. But growing up, my relatives made a trek to Disney World annually, as if it were a religious pilgrimage; the idea of depriving a kid of a trip to Disney was akin to child neglect. Plus, our hotel room was free. My mother was such a Disney devotee that she owned a timeshare.

The kids and I left the house around 4 p.m. for a 7 o'clock flight and drove to JFK Airport with time to spare. So far, so good. Except when I tried to check in at JFK using the kiosk, our flight didn't show up on the screen. I didn't think anything of it, and we got in line to

144

see an agent. When I handed her my license and flight number, she looked up at me and said, "This flight doesn't leave from Kennedy. It leaves from LaGuardia." LaGuardia is only 12 miles from JFK, but the traffic between airports was horrendous, and our flight took off in an hour. No other planes were leaving out of either airport that night with available seats. Worse, my mother had taken an earlier flight out of Philadelphia and was already en route. She was expecting us.

I turned to my kids and said, "Run!"

We took off, our bags clunking down two flights of stairs, and jumped in a cab. Then we sat in bumper-to-bumper traffic for half an hour, worrying whether we'd make the flight, which we did, with only minutes to spare. But the incident was a sign of my mental state at that point, in early March 2012, just over a year since Michael had been diagnosed with Tourette.

As for Disney World, it was hot. It was crowded. And it was not magical.

"This will probably be my last time here," my mother repeated several times during our stay, adding that she couldn't handle the walking anymore. I prayed it would be mine too: I had chosen to take a "vacation" in the least relaxing, most crowded place possible, when what I really needed to do was sit on a beach with a bucket of piña coladas. Clearly, Russ had been right about this one, as he was about many things.

By day three, I was having as much trouble walking as my mother. My knee, which had been bothering me for several years, had begun to flare up, and I fortified myself with Advil as I limped from Fantasyland to Tomorrowland and through several countries in Epcot. And in the end, the trip produced perhaps my favorite memory of Disney ever, as we were standing in a huge crowd watching the parade of princesses circling in front of Cinderella's castle. Just as the float carrying Snow White passed in front of us, Michael shouted "tits" loud enough for a gray-haired grandma standing next to him to hear. I still remember the look on her face: puzzled, then shocked, then appalled. I laughed at our inside joke and pretended I didn't hear a thing.

For whatever reason, that incident made me realize that I had turned a corner. Slowly, painfully, I had finally begun to accept that Michael might not fully recover in the near future. And I needed to teach him—and myself—how to accept himself as he was, at least for now.

When we returned home, an MRI confirmed a meniscus tear in my left knee, plus the scan showed I had arthritis and a herniated disc in my back. I was 47, but I felt 57. Not only was I in physical pain, but I felt emotionally drained too.

I was still teaching the college journalism class twice a week, a job I had to overprepare for since I didn't have teaching experience. I was also coediting a book with two former classmates from journalism school and filling in at Russ's office since his receptionist had quit without notice. Maybe these were all little things in a privileged life, but they added up, particularly when combined with the usual household errands and chores, carpooling, and volunteering. All the while I tried to make sure both of my kids, and especially Michael, stayed out of harm's way.

Even Bailey was giving me trouble. Our adorable puppy, who had already been kicked out of two dog-training courses, had now grown tall enough to jump on the kitchen island and nab food, and she was chewing on our new furniture to boot. When my knee gave out on me, it occurred to me that I had been so preoccupied with what Michael was going through that I hadn't given much thought to what I was going through. In the year I'd spent getting Michael back on track and making sure Katie didn't veer off course, I had lost my way. The worst part was a gnawing feeling of impending doom, partly due to two breast biopsies after suspicious spots were flagged on my mammograms. Both turned out to be benign, but I was still waiting for the other shoe to drop (as mom would say), and when it did, who would take care of the kids? And who would take care of me?

Naively, I had not expected the caregiver-mother role to be so damn exhausting or challenging despite my mother's warnings. I also hadn't expected that it would so completely hijack and redefine my identity, nor that my sense of self would become so wrapped up in my kids. Apart from my mother, nobody but me seemed to wonder or care how I managed to keep it all together and stay sane. Not that I was keeping it together or remaining exactly sane.

Three days after I finished grading my students' final exams, I had surgery on my knee. The doctor instructed me to rest and rehabilitate for several weeks, and with that permission, I proceeded to plop myself on the couch and do nothing. I think it was the first time I had stopped moving in a year and a half.

It's not that I had ignored my health completely. I had tried taking an antidepressant but hated the way it made me feel—bloated, sluggish, and sleepy. I got my mammograms, which necessitated the two scary biopsies. I tried yoga, Pilates, and a meditation video guided by an Australian woman whose soothing voice I found so unnerving that I couldn't sit through five minutes. I also signed up for a free session at a kickboxing gym. I thought it might release pent-up anger, and since I grew up with two brothers, I was proud of the fact that I could throw a punch (I'm a southpaw). Afterward, I was sore for three days.

The only habits that stuck were walking Bailey for "exercise" and my chocolate fix. I also treated myself to frequent doses of wine and, on especially tough days, bourbon. It was during that long, cold, achy winter of 2012 that I started drinking it on a regular basis.

I first developed a taste for whiskey on the day of my father's funeral, four years earlier. As I stood for hours in my black pumps in the receiving line, which snaked through the funeral home and into the parking lot, a well-coiffed blonde of about 65 shook my hand and said, "Your father introduced me to the Rusty Nail." About 20 minutes later, another woman said the same thing.

The next day, with family at a local restaurant, I decided to give my father's favorite drink a try. Besides whiskey, a Rusty Nail is made with a splash of Drambuie, a honey-flavored liquor that makes the brown liquid palatable for newbies like me.

Whiskey and its American cousin, bourbon, are an acquired taste, one my taste buds were schooled in after Michael was diagnosed with Tourette. On many nights that winter, Russ would come home from work and ask, "Big girl drink or little girl drink?" as he held two different-sized glasses.

Russ enjoyed mixing, shaking, and stirring, using his years of chemistry to create concoctions that helped him unwind after work and soothed my anxiety. I would be lying if I didn't admit it was a crutch and a coping mechanism, a reward after getting through another day. A bourbon Band-Aid.

At the time, Russ's stress level was also through the roof as he negotiated a contract with the hospital to buy his practice and dealt with several staffing issues at work. The most taxing was the departure of his relatively new hire, an ob-gyn who left the practice because she was so frazzled by the job.

This is not the part of the story where I recount how we sank into alcoholism. We stopped at one cocktail and maybe a glass of wine with dinner. The good news is that the habit enabled us to enjoy each other's company again. Our cocktail hour was like a mini, much-needed date night; Russ and I sat at the kitchen island while the kids did homework or watched TV. I think it made us feel normal. I had been yelling at Russ for years. I'm so soft-spoken that most people are surprised I am a screamer, but that's where my resentment took me. And now, on top of his long hours at work, Russ was also practicing one night a week for his David Bowie concert with School of Rock in late May.

But as Michael's condition began to improve, so did our relationship. With the help of a Rusty Nail or a Manhattan, Michael's Tourette felt manageable and even funny at times. We used to joke that the only job Michael could never do is become a CIA agent. Or librarian.

I needed our little happy hours to keep me going. That doesn't mean I was doing well, despite a community of caring friends and family. But it did help that Russ and I had some good friends in the tight-knit neighborhood where we lived, who were a blessing. Michael felt comfortable around them and continued to spend time at one neighbor's house in particular—without them, he would have been completely isolated. We even managed to throw the occasional dinner party (Russ's idea, because "life must go on"), and often, Michael would sit with the adults, chatting and ticcing, ticcing and chatting. My college friends, a group we referred to as the Hail Mary's, and who were like family, also checked in on me frequently and urged me to attend our annual girls' weekend in Rhode Island.

Our families were also supportive—Russ's mother was babysitting regularly, his sister referred me to one of the experts I consulted, and my other sister-in-law put me in touch with two people she knew who had kids with Tourette. And I talked to my own sister on the phone almost daily.

Having a friends-and-family hive was a good thing, because when I tried to attend a support group for parents of kids with Tourette, I found the experience incredibly emotional. Some of the parents had been dealing with Tourette for years, their young adult children saddled with serious comorbidities that made independent living impossible. When I recapped the meeting at home afterward, Russ said, "I don't think you're ready for this yet." He was right.

Talking one-on-one with other parents of kids with Tourette did help me cope. Early on, I spoke with several parents referred by the local TAA, and they were all very helpful and informative. And Helene Walisever remained a resource for years. Although I didn't stay active in our local chapter of the TAA, I did occasionally attend events, and I read everything the organization sent me. Looking back, I should have tried harder to meet and stay in touch with other parents of children with Tourette rather than just pumping them for information. As Walisever, who still runs the TAA's New York Hudson Valley Chapter's support groups, told me, "Talking to parents who get it and are nonjudgmental and can share their experiences of what worked and didn't is incredibly valuable."

I also relied on my faith during those early years, more than I had in decades, a turnabout I credit to my mother, who died in 2022. Until the pandemic, she went to church every day and prayed for Michael and our family. My own approach was to wait until I hit rock bottom to reach out to God. As Anne Lamott wrote in her book, *Help Thanks Wow: The Three Essential Prayers,* which came out, conveniently, just after Michael was diagnosed: "Prayer is talking to something or anything with which we seek union, even if we are bitter or insane or broken. (In fact, these are probably the best conditions under which to pray.)" The book remains on my bedside table.

There were so many moments when I couldn't see the light at the end of the tunnel. I had no idea how to get through the day, let alone figure out how to help Michael live a happy life. He was ticcing away, my marriage was a mess, and I worried about neglecting my other child. But in that darkness, I found angels—the people who showed up on my journey and held my hand.

I met some of them through a nonprofit called Smart Kids with Learning Disabilities. Talking to the parents of kids with any type of learning difference was encouraging and consoling, whether through the nonprofit or girlfriends who had kids with dyslexia, ADHD, autism, and other issues. They offered guidance, referred me to resources, shared books, and told me about their experiences with the public school system.

Although it wasn't clear yet whether Michael had a learning disability, commiserating with other parents of children who struggled was enormously comforting. Caregivers, I was learning, need a support system of their own.

Tourette experts have also come to recognize the challenges facing caregivers of children with Tourette and the need for family support as part of treatment protocols.

"We recognized that one of the biggest areas of struggle across the board, regardless of socioeconomic background, regardless of anything, is the stress that having a child or more than one child with Tourette puts on the family unit," said Dr. Coffman, who heads up Children's Mercy Kansas City, the highest-volume TAA Center of Excellence in the U.S. The program now has a full-time family therapist for people who come to the Tourette center—and there is a waiting list to see her.

"Parenting a child with Tourette is parenting beyond your wildest dreams—it's like advanced placement parenting," said Dr. Coffman, who has two children with Tourette himself. "There's no parenting book that explains what parenting a child with Tourette is like."

Smart Kids is all about empowering parents, helping them develop the skills they need to advocate for their children, and I decided to get more deeply involved, writing press releases for the group and helping with publicity. Along the way, I met mothers like me who had been told to lower their expectations for their children, and these mothers helped me gain confidence to fight to ensure Michael had the same opportunity to achieve as other children. It was as if these parents and Jane Ross, who founded Smart Kids, and all the many speakers I heard through the group had stood me in front of the mirror and given me the pep talk I needed as a parent.

Smart Kids also shifted my perspective in other ways, helping me to think of Tourette not in terms of deficits, but in terms of the strengths Michael might develop because of his condition. Focusing on a kid's strengths (in addition to addressing their weaknesses) "is just as important to their success in life and school," said Ross.

In the years since Michael was diagnosed, the term *neurodivergent* has become a catchall phrase to describe people whose brains function in a different way. Neurodiverse people might have autism, ADHD, dyslexia, or Tourette, but the fact that their brains are wired differently doesn't have to be a disadvantage. In fact, "twice exceptional," or 2E, is often used to describe students who are gifted and learning disabled. The idea that differences are not necessarily deficits is catching on in the Tourette community too.

When he spoke at the TAA's 50th anniversary gala in 2022, TAA Global Ambassador and journalist Aidy Smith said people with Tourette have a heightened sense of empathy, emotional intelligence, and cultural awareness. He told the audience gathered in New York City, filled with adults and children with Tourette: "We are these beautiful people, and we have these beautiful Tourette minds. We have all this energy that's moving around our bodies and coming out in the form of tics. But when we channel that energy into something we love doing, and when we find that passion, we become an unstoppable force of nature.... We need to reframe this conversation because Tourette is not a deficit, it is not a burden. It is a bloody superpower."

Years ago, Michael told me that he thought having Tourette "made him a better person." When I asked him about this recently, he said, "On a base level, it made me more sympathetic, because when you struggle and you go through being ostracized and bullied, you're not going to do it to anyone else. It makes you accepting and open to differences. It gave me perspective and made me thankful and aware that everything can go to shit. And it taught me about the ups and downs and to be grateful and that everyone has things going on that you don't know about. And to be nice—the biggest one is being nice."

Chapter 16

Meeting Mr. Right

In April, I'd traveled to D.C. to attend a TAA conference, and at 7 a.m., I walked into a seminar for the "newly diagnosed," my entire forehead feeling as if it were being squeezed by a vise.

I felt as if I were back in college. For one thing, I was hungover. I was in Washington, having stayed at my college roommate's house the night before, and we had dinner with several other friends, all of us eating, drinking, and chatting until past midnight. It felt so good to be away from home, having fun with people who knew me in my former life.

The prospect of an all-day lecture was not appealing, but I perked up when the speaker said, "It takes five minutes to get a Tourette diagnosis; it takes about six hours to know what it means, which is what we're going to do today."

The speaker was TAA Board of Directors member Dr. John Walkup. One of the subjects he focused on was co-occurring conditions common in kids with Tourette. He mentioned ADHD, OCD, anxiety disorders, bipolar disorder, and major depressive disorder in children with Tourette. Then, he showed a slide on all the insidious combinations kids can have. I had never heard of some of these scary symptoms, like rocking and flapping (called stereotypies), that made cursing seem not so bad.

Since Dr. Walkup's lecture, evidence has mounted that co-occurring features of Tourette are incredibly common. In 2015, a study was published in *JAMA Psychiatry* showing that 86% of people with Tourette will have at least one neuropsychiatric condition like ADHD, OCD, or anxiety on top of their tics, and that two-thirds of people with Tourette will have at least two comorbid conditions in addition to tics.

I felt relieved that we only had to deal with the tics as opposed to a grab bag of other issues. Michael did have anxiety, but it was mild, and he had just enough OCD to make it an asset. For example, he liked "everything to be in its proper place," as he had told Dr. King, and he often straightened up the house for me when it got messy.

An hour later, I looked up from scribbling furiously in my notebook to see Dr. Walkup still holding his tiny coffee cup from the bottom like some people hold a wineglass. He wore a striped shirt and blue striped tie, knotted off to the side like a schoolboy. He was so engaged and so fascinated by his own subject matter that I couldn't help but get excited too.

Though he stood at the front of the room, he chatted about Tourette as if we were colleagues at a workplace cocktail party, his tone authoritative, yet reassuring and friendly. He knew it all but didn't act like a know-it-all.

The most eye-opening and worrisome part of the lecture occurred when Dr. Walkup delved into details about how kids present with different

154

problems at different ages; while the severity of tics tended to decrease in early adulthood, the significance of some comorbidities climbed.

"The tic is the calling card to the doctor, but what I'm trying to get you guys to do is *not* get tic-focused. Focus on the whole child and focus on the co-occurring conditions that are associated with real impairment over the lifetime."

But what really got my attention was when he said that it was common to see ADHD, anxiety, and OCD in young kids with Tourette, followed by depression in teenagers.

"If your pediatrician says, "It's just a couple of tics; don't worry,' I'd say, "Can we monitor him over three, six, or nine months for symptoms of ADHD, anxiety, and OCD? Because when I see a tic, that clues me in to the fact that this youngster may have neurodevelopmental disturbances in other areas. I don't want to dismiss the tics because when I dismiss the tics, I'm dismissing the risk of what these other conditions might be and how they might affect the young person."

I thought back to all of the times we were told that Michael's tics were nothing to worry about. What would have happened if we had gotten him the right treatment earlier? As I sat there, I felt a tremendous sense of guilt that I hadn't pushed those early doctors harder, that I could have prevented this disaster.

I put on my reading glasses and pretended I was taking notes as my tears dripped onto the pages of my notebook.

What he said next made me look up: "Substance abuse is the dirty secret of Tourette." Then he wrinkled his face as if to say, "Sorry folks. You're screwed." Because what we all wanted to hear right then was that our child might turn to drugs or alcohol to tame their tics. In fact, when the TAA surveyed 281 adults with Tourette or tic disorders, 23% reported abusing substances, mostly alcohol.

"When teens with Tourette discover that their bodies quiet with marijuana and alcohol, it is really hard to convince them to not do that stuff," he continued. "They can get into a lot of trouble."

I was horrified to think that our situation could get worse. My mind began its usual trick, fast-forwarding to all the other potential problems that might arise over the next several years. It is not a pleasant feeling to have your mind racing at the same time your head is throbbing.

When I came back to the present, Dr. Walkup was saying, "I can't tell you how many parents I've seen dragging their kid to see the 30th doctor, but the dad's depressed, the mom's depressed, nobody's working, life is terrible, but they're gonna do everything they can to get Junior to see that next expert."

I had lost count of how many experts we had been to. And while my doctor confirmed that I was not clinically depressed, I was certainly stuck in a negative headspace. At least Russ was his usual glass-half-full self.

"And they haven't done the necessary stuff to take care of themselves or their marriage. Your kids will do fine if you put your own oxygen mask on first. Get the care you need, make sure your marriage is in decent shape. Your child depends upon you to be powerful and strong."

I felt as if he were talking directly to me. Michael—and Katie—had witnessed me falling to pieces, sobbing uncontrollably. They had heard Russ and me fighting. I wasn't sure myself that our marriage would make it.

I was the mom he was talking about. The one hell-bent on getting my son better but neglecting myself. And my marriage.

"Untreated parental psychopathology creates an environment that over the long haul is detrimental."

Ouch.

I knew I had been neglecting my marriage, but it was more or less intentional, kind of like a woman who feels a lump and pretends it's nothing because she doesn't want to know that she might have cancer. If I faced my issues head-on, I would either have to divert my attention from Michael and put some work into mending my marriage or walk away from someone I had built a life with, someone with flaws that were no worse than my own. I didn't want to know if our marriage was truly troubled or if it was just a temporary phase. I didn't want to talk about it, especially with a marriage therapist. And so, I ignored it.

That wasn't the only thing that resonated—and not in a good way. Dr. Walkup showed a slide titled "Problematic Assumptions" and then began to list some of the common excuses parents make for their kids' behavior: "He can't control it. He has a tough life. I want it easy for him. He needs special accommodations. Medication is the answer. It's all Tourette-related."

Oh, boy.

He sighed, then went on.

"Parents feel guilty. Once kids get a whiff of that...there's something that happens to families when they have a kid with Tourette," he said, putting his coffee cup down on the table. "They take three steps back." Then he raised his arms as if in surrender. "I don't know what to do," he said, mimicking a parent. "And in that vacuum, Junior knows what to do. He does whatever he dang well pleases! There's something about this condition that takes parents out of their game."

Oh, dear. I thought about all the times Russ had accused me of going too easy on Michael. I thought about all the times I tried to protect him.

"It's not about cutting these kids slack," Dr. Walkup said. "It's about developing a program to make them extremely competent despite their difficulties. It's a biological condition, like diabetes. And you can't just do insulin and forget about it. You have to do diet and exercise too. That's all we're saying."

He went on to talk about how parents shouldn't regard Tourette as a core part of a child's identity. "Though they probably can't control their motor movements, they do need to work really hard at controlling everything else they can and getting really good at it," he said. The point was to play up a million other things about the child, building an identity that goes beyond Tourette, so they can develop a sense of self that's not based on the disease, but on who they are as a person and what they want to make of themselves.

When I called Dr. Walkup in 2023, it was as if he picked up where he left off. When a child is suffering, he said, parents tend to lose track of the big picture. "Families become so wrapped up in the Tourette diagnosis at age 9, 10, 11, and 12 that they form that as the basic identity. And so when they're 20 and their tics are gone, they say, 'I have Tourette syndrome, but I'm not ticcing anymore, and I don't know who I am, I don't know what I'm about, I don't know where I'm going, because somebody made me a poster child for Tourette syndrome,'" he told me.

"When the going gets tough, think about the natural course, and the natural course is for it to get better or go away," he said.

He told me the criteria for a Tourette diagnosis had changed drastically in recent years. The conventional wisdom was that most kids had what are known as transient, or provisional, tics—which is what we were told. In the past, kids were much more likely to be diagnosed with a provisional tic disorder even if they ticced for eight months of the year but didn't for four months and did the same the following year and the year after, he explained. Whereas now, if a child has their first tic at age 6 and still has tics at age 8, they should be diagnosed with a chronic tic disorder because it persisted for more than a year.

It was a bit confusing, but the takeaway, in my mind, was that for a long time doctors had been too dismissive of kids with tics like Michael who ended up having Tourette.

Now, more than a decade after Michael's diagnosis, I have come to realize that when it comes to Tourette, a lot of information is fluid and evolving—even how various tic disorders are defined. When I looked into what differentiates a chronic tic disorder from Tourette syndrome, I learned that, in addition to Tourette syndrome, the *DSM-5-TR* identified persistent (chronic) motor or vocal tic disorder, provisional tic disorder, other specified tic disorder, and unspecified tic disorder.

And there are many nuances. For example, Amanda Talty explained that a lot of people with Tourette syndrome are diagnosed as having a tic disorder as opposed to Tourette because "they don't fall into the small box that is the *DSM* criteria." One example of this conundrum is that if you don't have an observable tic that is the same for more than a year, then you don't have Tourette syndrome, according to the *DSM*. "It doesn't matter if you have tics all year long, and your tics change, and you have motor and vocal tics," said Talty.

She added that how it is defined has led to "an underrepresentation of Tourette syndrome," in part because "clinicians strictly interpret the diagnostic criteria or just do not know enough about Tourette syndrome to spot it when they see it." This is one explanation for why the numbers have shifted upward over the years. The one in 160 statistic I read back when Michael was first diagnosed has been adjusted over the years to reflect the reality that a lot more Americans have Tourette and tic disorders than once thought, although many remain undiagnosed.

In 2022, there was another big change. That's when the TAA asked the CDC to revisit the prevalence of Tourette. After looking at previously published review articles that used meta-analysis (groups of studies) to calculate estimates of Tourette and persistent tic disorders, the CDC estimated that 2.1% to 2.4% of children ages 5 to 14 years had a persistent tic disorder, including Tourette syndrome. It turns out that people of color may not be underrepresented either—they just weren't sampled appropriately.

That translates to one in 50 children. That's a far cry from one in 160.

"This is not a rare condition. This is not a condition that should be in the shadows," is what Talty told listeners at the 2022 TAA Supporting Abilities Gala. "This is a condition that, like so many others, deserves the resources, funding, and research that it deserves."

Less than 10% of kids with Tourette, she told us, move into adulthood with severe symptoms. That was incredibly reassuring, since I'd heard early on that only a third outgrow it entirely. (Jump ahead a decade and these numbers have also been adjusted based on studies showing that remission is more common in adulthood).

Dr. Walkup later explained the number of people with persistent, severe Tourette is "really small" and tends to occur in the context of comorbidities or challenging life experiences. "That is unusual because the natural course is for it to get better or even sometimes go away. That's what's supposed to happen unless something intervenes to keep it going," he said. "When I hear about teenagers and adults who are having worsening tics, there's something going on that needs to be identified."

When I looked into this further, Dr. Leckman agreed that severe cases of long-term Tourette remain a mystery. "What's fascinating is the vast majority of individuals who have tics really only have them in childhood, and they are not very severe, and they're hardly noticeable. Then you have a smaller and smaller number of individuals who go on to have more classic cases of Tourette, and then you have an unfortunate few who go on to have persistent dreadful tics for much of their life," he said. "That's one of the things we have struggled with in terms of finding interventions."

Looking back, other experts had assured us that many, if not most, kids with Tourette improve over time, and they advised a similar tack in terms of focusing on Michael's strengths. But it took more than a year for this truth to sink in.

I remembered that Tony Mullen had also recommended that the number one rule of good parenting is to figure out what makes your child tick. "Parents need to accept their children, appreciate who they are, figure out their strengths and weaknesses, and help them discover what they want to do in life," Tony said. "This will prevent behavioral problems and engage and motivate students to perform at a higher level of academic performance than they thought possible."

As I sat in the audience at the TAA lecture, every decision I had ever made about Michael raced through my mind. I felt like an Olympic judge tallying my good-mother score.

And I definitely wasn't getting a 10. I had plucked our son out of our well-regarded but enormous public school system in seventh grade and transferred him to a hippie school with no tests or grades. I had let him stop therapy. Although he was taking three medications (Lexapro, Geodon, and Tenex), I had chosen not to enroll him in a medical study conducted by some of the top researchers in the field, and not to give CBIT a real try. And I had focused so much of my time and energy on my son that I allowed my marriage and my own well-being to suffer. (My 10-year-old daughter appeared unscathed so far, but who knew?)

At the same time, this doctor was standing here, coffee cup still in hand, saying that I had done at least one thing right by encouraging Michael's musical talents. I had also found a new school where he had a new group of friends and seemed to be thriving. Last but not least, the ticcing was under control, and if he did feel the need to tic at school, Michael could roam the halls freely, and he wasn't afraid of what the kids would think.

I had walked in that morning, hungover and feeling like a horrible parent, but I walked out invigorated. It was a huge step toward helping me trust my own instincts.

Chapter 17

The Lucky Break

In April, Michael's first report card from the hippie school arrived in the mail.

When Russ came home from work, we stood at the kitchen island, no drinks this time, and read it together. We were four months into this expensive experiment, and we were both anxious to know if it was working.

The report card began with an overview of "individual and community goals." Michael had set individual goals when he transferred, and they included "a new level of independence and self-confidence, greater self-knowledge, and more effective self-expression."

The community goals were "to build a meaningful place in a community of peers and a larger community."

One of us cracked a joke, saying that it was a modern-day commune made up of 12- and 13-year-olds.

162

Each teacher was allotted a full page to evaluate the student. The language arts teacher commented on how well Michael had adjusted to the new school and said he fit in socially, engaged in class, and had learned to advocate for himself. She pointed out that there was a lot of in-class conversation, and Michael was highly energized by these connections.

I raised my eyebrows, a bit surprised by this unprecedented praise.

The only negative comment was that Michael had turned in 9 of the 26 language arts assignments late.

"You think someone would have told me?" I said to Russ, wondering what the repercussions would be in a school with no grades.

The "expressive arts" page outlined the school's philosophy, which I read aloud. "Children who participate in art, body, drama, movement, and music activities within a school setting experience increased motivation for learning in other areas, as well as a sense of themselves as human beings at their very core."

The report card reinforced how different this institution was from the Catholic school I'd attended, where priests and nuns still wore their habits and collars. My seventh-grade teacher, a lifeguard in Atlantic City in the summer, was so strict he would whack students with an oar in front of the entire class if they misbehaved (I was spared the embarrassment).

In contrast, students at Michael's school called teachers by their first names and took a weekly "values class," where they met to discuss issues of concern and to "clarify individual and group values." I wouldn't have characterized the place as a school full of misfits, but a lot of the kids didn't—or didn't want to—fit in at mainstream schools. I'd heard through the grapevine that one girl came home from a tour of the school and announced to her mother, "I have found my people."

That was more or less how Michael felt too. The hippie school housed a small, insular tribe, and our son was relieved to be accepted by them. One of the things he liked best was that there were no cliques. The school staff went out of their way to ensure everyone was included—for instance, by making sure all students were invited to every birthday party or bar mitzvah.

When we finally got to math on page 10, we read every word. The stand-ins for grades were that the student had demonstrated *exposure*, *experience*, or *fluency*. Michael scored *fluency* or *experience* in all of the math categories, the equivalent of A's and B's. The teacher's conclusion: "Overall, you have made a successful transition to our pre-algebra program."

After all of Michael's troubles in math, it was a huge relief. As much as we mocked the school and its unconventional ways, its magic seemed to be working. Even Russ seemed OK with it as long as they also taught the basics of reading, writing, and arithmetic.

Russ paused to mix a shaker of celebratory Manhattans. I grabbed a bowl of cashews, and we sat down on the couch.

This first report card gave us hope that the hippie school was the right choice—that it would give Michael the support and confidence he needed to put his self-esteem issues to rest.

He was learning to become community minded and self-aware, to identify his strengths and weaknesses, and to like and appreciate his uniqueness. Could I ask for anything more from a school? Apparently, yes, but we would not learn that lesson for another year.

"Mom, do you know how John Bonham died?" Michael asked one day as we listened to music in the car. I knew that Bonham had been Led Zeppelin's legendary drummer and that he had died an early death, but I didn't know the cause.

Michael's next School of Rock show, which he began practicing right after Black Sabbath, was Led Zeppelin, and apparently, he had been boning up on trivia.

"He got drunk and choked on his own vomit."

This was not necessarily information I wanted my 12-year-old son to know, but I reminded myself that he was enamored with the music, not the rock 'n' roll lifestyle. At least not yet.

"Whole Lotta Love." "Heartbreaker." "Black Dog." "The Ocean." "Good Times, Bad Times." He practiced these Zeppelin songs over and over, learning the lyrics and the guitar and bass parts. He taught himself the drum solos even though he wouldn't be playing them (that would come later). And though he didn't really know how to read music, he could play the chords, and during his lessons, his instructor would fine-tune his performance.

I had never seen my son so focused. Music was all he cared about. When Michael created his first Facebook profile, under "Religion," he listed "rock 'n' roll."

He sat for hours at his new drum set, practicing beneath a poster of John, Paul, George, and Ringo. When he wasn't downstairs practicing, he was talking about music. During our weekly drives to School of Rock, Michael liked to ponder whether he should live in Los Angeles or New York when he grew up, weighing the pros and cons of each city in terms of his music career and lifestyle. "L.A. has Hollywood and beaches, but New York has more hipster bands," he'd say. "Plus, New York City is close to home." I liked that he still wanted to live near his parents when he grew up.

I taught my class on Tuesdays and Thursdays, so on those days I would drive more than an hour each way to teach, pick up Michael at school on my way home, greet Katie after she got off the bus, then drive Michael another 20 minutes back to New Canaan for band practice. After that, I drove home and made dinner, and three hours later I picked him up.

People asked all the time if I dreaded all that driving, but I relished those car rides with Michael. We played classic rock stations constantly. The Rolling Stones. The Who. Bruce. Creedence. The Dead. I knew the words to all the songs, and he did too. "You used to call this 'old people music,'" I teased him. Now, he couldn't get enough.

Hearing Michael's prepubescent voice belting out the music of my own teenage years drew us even closer. Oftentimes, he also practiced his songs, which is why I now know most of the words to almost every Led Zeppelin song he ever played onstage.

As we sat in rush hour traffic, we had ample time to chat. Week after week, we talked and talked as he flipped through the stations on the radio, commenting on the songs and bands. I encouraged his dream of becoming a rock star, but I also assumed it was a childhood fantasy akin to a toddler wanting to become a firefighter after a tour of the local station.

I truly supported his decision to pursue a career in the music industry. At the same time, I knew he had other gifts locked inside of him. It bothered me that he was so much smarter than I was yet was being held back by a disability. I wanted him to rise above it like the neurodivergent author Patricia Polacco and have the choice of any career path.

Granted, if my son had said he wanted to join the circus, I would have asked, "Do you want to be a clown or tightrope walker?" Another tip from Tony Mullen, the star teacher I'd interviewed, was: "You can't help a child realize their potential if they are following *your* dreams." I wanted to support Michael in whatever he was passionate about, to make him feel better about himself. That's what Dr. King had been hinting at when he asked Michael about his hobbies, and what Dr. Walkup had urged parents to do at the conference in Washington.

I liked to joke that I was probably the only mother in our ultra-competitive, tony town who encouraged their kid to become a rock star. I couldn't forget Dr. Walkup's words about needing to find something your kid is good at, instead of just going along with the crowd. By now it had sunk in.

By the day of Michael's first Led Zeppelin show, just past his 13th birthday, my son had a case of the jitters. But as we walked into the Lucky Break, which was just as dingy as I remembered it, I felt like an old hand—a mom groupie. Over the past weeks we'd gotten to know the parents and the kids, so Russ and I ordered a beer and started mingling.

But when Michael picked up his guitar and began playing his group's first song—"Good Times, Bad Times"—Russ and I moved to the front to get the best photos. Michael wore jeans and a baggy T-shirt with a *Life Is Good* logo and a drawing of a guitar. He was barely five feet tall, still chubby, and as he played, he jerked his head to the side a good 25 times to sweep his long bangs out of his eyes. To my eyes he resembled a prepubescent Bobby Sherman, the '70s pop star.

While I enjoyed watching Michael on guitar, I loved hearing him sing even more. When he began playing "Heartbreaker," my favorite, Russ and I laughed out loud at the racy lyrics—coming from the mouth of a babe. The other parents in the audience were singing along, or mouthing the words, and some were clearly amused too.

But when Michael's eyes peeked out from under his veil of bangs, his gaze was resolute. Playing guitar took him someplace else. We'd known since the choral concert in Carnegie Hall that Michael didn't tic when he sang. But now he was losing himself in his music, just like James Durbin. I didn't know where he went or what he thought, but I knew that for him, it was a release, an escape, and a salvation.

Michael's voice hadn't changed yet, and he could easily hit the high notes—a tenor just like Robert Plant. Clearly, music had become central to Michael's existence and, by extension, ours. Russ was now singing in the Bowie band, and we were regularly going to hear live music, something we had enjoyed when we were young but hadn't done much of in recent years. Music was helping my marriage too.

But if I had to select one moment when I glimpsed my son coming into his own, it was in that dirty old bar. When I look at the pictures and videos we took that day, I don't see a boy with Tourette. What I saw that night was a rock 'n' roller, and it made me believe that everything might be OK.

As Bruce Springsteen, my musical idol and fellow New Jersey native, once said, "The first day I can remember looking into a mirror and being able to stand what I saw was the day I had a guitar in my hand."

I had tried everything to find a cure for our son. It turns out that the miracle I had been looking for had been in our basement all along: a cheap guitar in the corner, gathering dust.

Chapter 18

A Special Education

The fall of Michael's eighth-grade year brought more difficult choices—namely, where Michael would attend high school. Most of the kids at his school seemed to be headed to private high schools, but whether Michael would follow that path or return to the public school system depended on his eligibility for special education services. Without them, I was apprehensive about sending him to a place with 2,800 students and few accommodations aside from a 504 Plan. As for Michael, he refused to even go on a tour of the local high school. In his mind, it represented his old life, his "something is wrong with me" life.

I, too, wanted to find a safe space for our son—a nurturing environment where he could hone his skills and interests like music and acting and develop new interests too. A school where Michael might write himself a happy ending.

So, the two of us made a deal: I would take him to visit any private high school in the area as long as he would agree to apply to a local all-boys Jesuit school, which had been on my radar for some time, especially since Russ and I had both attended a Jesuit university.

At one school we visited, a five-person ensemble was playing jazz inside a small amphitheater in the front of the building. As we entered, the headmaster greeted each of us, shaking our hands, looking into our eyes, and holding our gaze for two extra seconds as she said in a British accent, "Welcome. It's *so* nice to meet you." I had warned Michael about the handshaking; I'd heard about it from another parent. To my relief, he stuck out his hand like a pro. Then a well-spoken, cute girl in a short skirt, part of the school uniform, who seemed incredibly sophisticated for her age, gave us a tour.

"I love it!" Michael said on the way home.

Who wouldn't? It was where the wealthiest, coolest kids from his school ended up, plus the classes were small, the teachers engaged, and the girls pretty. In fact, everyone looked perfect.

I walked away thinking that the last place Michael needed to be was at a school where he felt different. That night, having our customary cocktail, Russ made a point that stuck with me like a lawyer's closing argument in a packed courtroom.

"I graduated 53rd in a class of 183 students in my high school. I didn't try my hardest," he said. "When I got to college, I told myself, 'If I want to become a doctor, I can't get A minuses and B's.'"

I sipped my drink, only half-listening to his little lecture, feeling a fight brewing.

"Michael has been through hell, and I am hell-bent on making sure he gets a good education," I retorted.

"This is not just about his Tourette—he has an attitude problem," Russ shot back. "He can go to the best school in the country, but if he doesn't change his attitude, he won't thrive. How much is Tourette

170

and how much is taking personal responsibility? He needs to wake up and realize he has to work hard to get ahead in life."

Maybe he has a point, I thought. It had always frustrated Russ that Michael didn't apply himself. And I was complicit in coddling our son. We had given him every advantage, stretching our budget and sacrificing our retirement funds to pay for his education. So many kids don't get those opportunities. Was he going to waste them?

"He uses his intelligence to get what he wants," Russ continued, warming to his subject. "He has to learn that if he wants to be successful, he has to get his ass in gear."

For years, Russ had been trying to figure out how to light a fire in Michael, to stoke a passion for learning. So far, the spark had not ignited.

Then he said something that made me feel really bad.

"You're overwhelmed by all of these decisions and parenting him. So am I. I stress about paying bills. I haven't slept. I don't mean to be dismissive. I am trying to be objective. I am overwhelmed by the financial aspect and the emotional stress. I have too many balls in the air."

I knew he was right. The right attitude, plus his drive, got my husband into Cornell Medical School. He worked hard then, and he still did. I admired that. I didn't want Michael to turn into a spoiled kid with no work ethic.

Yet my instinct was to keep doing exactly what Dr. Walkup said parents do after a Tourette diagnosis: make excuses for my son and let him rule the roost. If I kept it up through high school, what would become of him?

In Italy, there's a word for a mama's boy: *mammone*. Sometimes I worried that Michael would be living at home until he was 30, with me making his dinner and doing his laundry.

After my conversation with Russ, I read Michael the riot act. I told him that if we spent the money to send him to private school, and he didn't do well, we would pull him out and he would go straight to the public school. He said he was ready to start trying. I decided to put off the decision until after we learned where he was accepted. Meanwhile, I tried to figure out how our family could come up with the cash and began applying for part-time jobs as well as looking for steady freelance work.

Russ surprised me by coming on a few school visits and attending all the parent interviews, where he was able to sum up Michael's strengths and challenges succinctly and warmly. He also made an enthusiastic case for why Michael was a strong candidate for these schools. "When Michael was diagnosed," he said, "we realized that public school was a poor fit. Now we want to find an environment where he can flourish like he has in the past year."

He sounded so sincere that I had to think he was warming up to the idea. Either that or he was appeasing me.

In the end, Michael applied to three private schools, including the Jesuit school I had been gunning for and that Russ was in favor of—especially since it was half the cost of other private schools. Michael said, "I don't want to go to an all-boys school. I don't want to go to a *Catholic* school."

Our son may not have been convinced, but I was. In the parent essay, I mentioned all of my Catholic creds; the fact that Russ and I had met at a Jesuit university; that after graduation I joined the Jesuit Volunteer Corps in Los Angeles to work in a homeless shelter; and that we were married by a Jesuit priest. I also mentioned that in a challenging, supportive high school environment, Michael could continue to blossom, even without special education services. Finally, I wrote that we trusted the Jesuits to not only educate our son, but guide and inspire him on his journey into adulthood.

This was my Hail Mary pass, my last-ditch effort to help Michael stay the course.

~

The student center at our local high school is a one-acre room with five sets of doors leading into five separate "houses," like in Harry Potter. Part cafeteria, part student hangout, part stage, this was the place to see and be seen, before the eyes of 2,800 peers. Michael refused to even step inside.

"Everyone says it's much better than the middle school," I tried, though I wasn't convinced.

"I hate the kids there."

"We hate things, but we don't hate people," I said, repeating the words I taught my kids when they were young. Sometimes my lectures annoyed me too.

I went on the tour alone.

I kept thinking back to a conversation I'd had with a woman months before. I'd been out for a friend's birthday, where I met a mom with kids older than mine, one of whom had gotten addicted to drugs while he attended the local public high school.

She painted a picture of a lawless landscape where lost kids wandered haplessly as dark forces tugged at them, luring them into mischief and misbehavior. Worse, she said the school was full of bullies who physically and mentally abused weaker kids.

When I shared my dilemma, she was unequivocal that sending Michael to the public high school would prove disastrous. Her words stuck with me: "They'll eat him alive."

When I learned that the school motto was "Freedom with responsibility," I admitted I did not yet trust my son to make good choices, though I wanted to. And after what I had learned about the adolescent brain, I was worried that his still-developing frontal lobe would make him vulnerable to every temptation.

As I strolled through the corridors of the high school, which stretched a full half mile from one end to the other, I thought that

Michael *would* get lost there, literally and figuratively. Contemplating that, I looked up and found myself before a set of double doors, which I learned was the Resource Room, for students receiving special education services.

"May I take a peek?" I asked.

If on one side of the doors was Rydell High, with hallways as boisterous and chaotic as a superhighway, the other side was a sanctuary—an empty, quiet space with no commotion. Any child with an IEP would be able to access this space, and if Michael was going to attend this school, he needed to get inside these magic doors.

The first step toward getting Michael special education services was a PPT meeting. Before that, I had requested the meeting back in September; before that, there were forms to fill out, and Michael's school had to complete and send a packet of information on him. In addition, I sent reams of information about Michael's medical history. Then a special education teacher spent two days observing Michael in the classroom setting at his hippie school. She also evaluated his reading, writing, math, and spelling proficiency, among other skills.

I was cautiously optimistic that Michael would end up being eligible for special education services. For one thing, the teacher who observed Michael was from a different town, where the hippie school was located, not the town where we lived, so she had no skin in the game, so to speak—she would not be biased against making the public school pay for what Michael needed. I also told myself that the school district had a $140 million budget, the highest in the state. Couldn't they afford to shell out some of it for my child?

The PPT meeting took place in late November. Russ and I filed through the metal detector and checked in at the security desk, where I surreptitiously reached into my purse, broke off a chunk of chocolate, and slipped it into my mouth. It was 9 a.m. In addition to Russ and me, there was a representative from the hippie school, plus several other staff members from the town education department.

There was even a representative from Michael's old public middle school on a conference line.

At the meeting, I read aloud a letter from Dr. King as well as a statement I had prepared beforehand, since I worried my nerves would get the best of me if I tried to speak off the cuff. I explained Michael's medical history and described his diagnosis, adding that though he would sometimes tic out of the blue in stressful situations, the full-blown curse words had been replaced by muffled sounds and minor motor tics like eye blinking.

Then I summed up Michael's middle school experience—his difficulties socially, emotionally, and academically—and how he had switched his math grade to pass/fail in seventh grade. I acknowledged that he did not have any special accommodations in his current school but pointed out that there were also only about seven students per class.

My audience sat stone-faced, apparently unmoved by my words or anything I presented. Whatever I said, however much I argued, Michael would either be eligible for an IEP or not, based on their own criteria. We had done everything we could. Now all we could do was wait.

Meanwhile, there were inklings that Michael also knew that high school would be a make-or-break time for him. One day, I sat down at my desk and noticed nearly a dozen windows open on my computer: Middlebury College, Colorado College, Bard, NYU, Syracuse, Georgetown, Bates, and the University of Pennsylvania. There was also a link to a list of "hipster colleges." That gave me a chuckle.

Later, I said, "I know you are smart enough, but you're going to have to start studying in high school if you want to get into any of those colleges."

"I will."

I pointed out the obvious but tried to make light of it. "Ya know..." I said, "you haven't really tried very hard in middle school."

"Well, maybe I'm ready to start trying," he said for the second time in recent months.

Aside from making some genuine friends, appearing more relaxed, and ticcing less often and intensely, something else happened during the spring of seventh grade, something that suggested that Michael truly was becoming his own person: He became a vegetarian after two of his close friends, twin boys and lifelong vegetarians themselves, convinced Michael to watch a documentary. In it, Paul McCartney, one of Michael's musical heroes and an outspoken vegetarian himself, talked about everything from the inhumane treatment of animals in the meat industry to the health benefits of a diet without meat.

Russ, Katie, and I guessed he would stick with it for a week, maybe two. After all, this was a child who asked for chicken wings when we ordered pizza, a hungry, growing boy who liked a hearty, meat-laden meal. Michael's grandmothers were especially flummoxed. Every time they saw him or talked to me, they would ask, "Is he still a vegetarian?" as if he had a bad cold. Worse, the entire neighborhood joked that they were placing bets on how long he'd last. But Michael, who had until then shied away from anything that might brand him as different, became more vigilant.

Forgoing meat indicated resilience and a level of maturity and self-acceptance I hadn't seen before, along with a willingness to set himself apart from the crowd. I credited those changes to the environment at the hippie school, where, among other things, he learned to think critically. While it wasn't a complete panacea, the school laid the groundwork for the next chapter in his life.

Then a curious thing happened: A month after Michael stopped eating meat and hit the health food hard, he stopped ticcing almost completely, his movements and vocalizations now a whisper compared to a shout.

It made me rethink having given up on the elimination diet so readily. It turns out there's plenty of evidence that dietary changes can quell tics. According to the book *Natural Treatments for Tics & Tourette's*, avoiding foods that might be triggers, like sugar, caffeine, and artificial additives, as well as adding nutrient-packed foods to boost brain and body function, made good sense. Michael was doing both.

What struck me about this newfound dietary vigilance was that Michael didn't seem worried about what anyone else was saying about his new choice. Two years before, he wouldn't wear his Converse sneakers to school because a few kids had made fun of him. Now he wore his vegetarianism like a medal because he felt it was the right thing to do.

When I look back at this period, becoming a vegetarian wasn't only important because the tics were silenced; it was important because he was finally able to stand up for something he believed in. He brushed off the barbs and didn't seem to care that he was different. And if he could do that, at 13, it gave me hope that he would continue to cope with his condition and any other challenges life flung at him. Maybe he wouldn't get eaten alive at the public high school after all.

When the report arrived from the special education department, the evaluator wrote that during her observation, Michael had coughed, rubbed his nose, and "tapped the top of the table with his hand"—in other words, he drummed. But it did not disrupt the other students.

More important, we learned that all of Michael's test scores were above average. Michael was observed participating in class discussions, he answered the teachers' questions when called upon, he read "smoothly and accurately," and his comments were "perceptive and indicative of Michael's high-order thinking ability."

So, no learning disability, no IEP. I was not surprised, but I was disappointed. Michael would have to either go to the high school without extra help, never seeing the resource room behind the magic doors, or he would attend one of the three private high schools we'd applied to.

It was true that Michael was doing better overall, thriving at School of Rock—his latest show was Pink Floyd—and happy with the hippie school, where they were making go-carts for a science project and rehearsing for an upcoming Shakespeare performance of, again, *A Midsummer Night's Dream*.

But I worried that, in our public high school, with no or few accommodations, progress would be short-lived. I worried that everything would be a challenge for him—and me. I would need to pony up and tap TAA resources, utilize Smart Kids, find mentors and allies, and hire an education advocate to guide us.

I would have to become even more of an expert, his champion and advocate, and figure out ways to make public school work as thousands of parents with limited resources did every year for their kids with learning disabilities and other differences. I could do it, but I was already struggling to keep things together, even with our privilege and the connections I'd already made.

Looking back, I should have been more relieved to learn that Michael did not have a learning disability—a blessing, given how many kids with Tourette do. And it does seem curious, even to me, that I was hell-bent on getting the IEP at the same time I was willing to pay tens of thousands a year to send him to a private school that wouldn't provide accommodations. By then, I had come to believe, for better or worse, that I was the only one really looking out for him.

A few weeks later, Michael was denied admission at his first-choice private high school, wait-listed at school number two, and accepted at the Jesuit school. I sent the deposit the next day.

Michael protested a bit, but Russ assured him that the Jesuits were the "cool Catholics." Besides, he was preoccupied with practicing for School of Rock's upcoming "Best of Season" show, which would feature two songs from each of the four local programs. It was the first time he was selected to perform, and he would be playing guitar on the Pink Floyd song "Run Like Hell."

Things were looking up. Then in late May, a week after Michael's 14th birthday, I got a letter from his new school informing us that Michael would be placed in Algebra 1 for his freshman year math class—the same level he'd taken at the hippie school. I knew he'd completed a math placement test a few weeks earlier, and I was sure there must have been a mistake. After all, his last report card from the hippie school had said he was on track. We'd had several parent-teacher meetings. There were no red flags.

When I inquired further, I learned that Michael had answered only 11 of 40 questions on the placement test correctly. The chair of the math department in his new school said she had reviewed the math records the hippie school had sent over, which contained a checklist of topics that Michael was supposedly proficient in. Only he wasn't. "His retention of those topics and ability to use those skills has certainly declined," the chair of the math department in the Catholic school said diplomatically. Did he ever develop those skills in the first place? Without tests or grades, who knew?

Meanwhile, Russ and I tried to figure out how this could have happened. Was it all the time he had spent rehearsing for the school play? Or had his elective classes in photography, clay, yoga, and Pilates taken up too much of his attention?

I thought, *Was it naïve to think that if we were to pay $34,000 a year, he would not have to retake algebra? Or could Tourette be affecting his ability to learn more than I'd realized, despite the tests indicating he has no learning disability?*

I remember looking at my husband and thinking, *You were right.* And now Michael was exactly where he would have been if he had been demoted at the public middle school. So maybe that witchy math teacher was right too. And we would have saved 50 grand. To his credit, Russ didn't say, "I told you so."

In June we attended Michael's middle school graduation. I had been told that in addition to all the hugging, it would be an incredibly moving experience, so I clutched my Kleenex as I waited for the ceremony to begin. One by one, the graduating students stood up and spoke about what the school meant to them. In his speech, Michael said, "At my old school, most students tried to fit in, but here, I finally feel comfortable because I don't feel like I have to try to fit in. People are accepted for being different."

Apropos to the occasion, at a reception after the graduation ceremony, Michael did a guitar solo and sang the Green Day song "Good Riddance."

I think we were all ready to move on from middle school.

Chapter 19

The Good Things in Life

Back home after the morning graduation ceremony, I sat down at my computer and sent Russ an email.

I was upset about the math debacle, emotional about graduation, and miffed about a new development: Russ had informed me that he was taking Michael to London the following week, to a music festival in Belgium. Russ's cousin would be hosting; almost everything except airfare and food would be free. Yes, I was jealous, but my main gripe was that his cousin had suggested what I considered to be a cockamamie plan to leave Michael alone—at 13—in a hotel room so that he and Russ could go out at night. I got that some people might be OK with that, but I was concerned (and again, maybe a bit jealous). I unloaded a lot more for good measure—how Russ took me for granted, never made me a priority, all the things that had been bugging me for years.

181

Sending my husband emails may seem strange, but writing to Russ was sometimes easier than talking to Russ. Our in-person conversations usually ended in an argument unrelated to why either of us had been angry in the first place. "You spend more time with our dog than with me!" I would say, thinking of how, when Russ got home, he went straight to Bailey to pet her before saying hi to the kids or me. "But you don't greet me at the door wagging your tail," he would say, which always made me laugh.

Looking back, my anger waxed and waned like Michael's tics.

Tourette didn't necessarily cause the problems in our marriage. The sometimes petty grievances and nitpicky criticisms (I'll admit, mostly mine) had chipped away at something integral to our relationship, which had fractured with the stress of the past two years. Michael's illness felt like the straw that broke the camel's back on top of all our other problems: Russ's unending workload, my feelings of neglect, and yes, years of financial strain. Now, everything we had built was in danger of collapsing.

In the email, I wrote that I was willing to take part of the blame but resented that I was the only one who acknowledged that ours was a broken relationship. If I felt that way, it should matter. In his reply, he pointed out that neither of us had been very good at communicating our grievances.

"Sometimes I feel that I get 90% of the blame while you get 10%. I would be happy to take the lion's share, but I feel like you need to acknowledge your own responsibility."

In retrospect, I think we both wanted our feelings validated.

He also suggested we book a weekend away without the kids for my birthday in August.

"I would be thankfull to have the time alone with you," he wrote.

"Thankful is spelled with one L," I responded.

I couldn't help correcting him. Which made me realize that he was, in fact, not wholly to blame.

After Michael came back from London, something shifted. My son seemed more mature, independent, and honestly, a bit less needy. And he'd had a fabulous trip with his father filled with music and new memories to cherish. Russ had been right again.

Something shifted in Russ too. He told me he had signed up to receive emails from an online marriage counselor. Neither one of us felt enthusiastic about marriage counseling, but this DIY approach seemed like a positive, if surprising, step that gave me hope. And I did notice a change in his behavior. Besides making more of an effort to understand and accommodate my feelings, he was more attentive, more engaged, and expressed more interest in my life, my feelings, and my opinion.

After 23 years of marriage, Russ became much more lavish with his praise of me, or, as he says, "appreciative of the things that make you, you."

And I finally allowed myself to stop stewing.

As we eased into a period of relative harmony, it occurred to me that maybe I was the one who had erased Russ from the picture, when all along, he was more involved and invested in family decisions than I admitted. I had felt alone at times during these past few years, but some of that was because I had shut him out.

Another turning point occurred around that time when I got rejected from a well-paying gig I had applied for. Michael noticed I was upset, put his hand on mine, and repeated something I had said to him over and over to help him get through his medical crisis: "Think about all the good things in your life."

I did. I was so grateful for my health, my family, and my husband. And I wanted to be more appreciative of the things that made Russ who he was: the fact that when he came home at night, he was usually in a good mood, even after working a 20-hour shift, first in the office and then overnight in the hospital.

When I vented to Russ, he listened and weighed in. He was particularly good at helping me make decisions, especially when I felt overwhelmed. And he had always been unfazed by Michael's

Tourette, which ensured that at least one of us remained rational during our many crises.

I thought about how Russ, though he worked longer hours than I did, still managed to cook elaborate meals for us on the weekends and take care of our yard, including planting a vegetable garden with the kids. He also taught them to ski and fish. And he doled out a lot of money we didn't have at the time because I insisted our son needed a private school.

He had been my foundation all along, and a rock-solid one. I just hadn't realized it.

Russ and I did go away for my birthday, to the North Fork of Long Island, where we rented bikes, went to a few local wineries, and had dinner out. There was no shortage of things to talk about, and nothing to fight about, and his positive qualities shone through: Russ can not only be the life of the party, but he is so informed about so many subjects. I love the way he can talk to anybody, how he takes interest in everyone's life stories. And his glass-half-full view counters my doomsday one.

It was getting easier to remember why I had married him in the first place. In fact, back in May, when he had sung in School of Rock's Bowie show, it brought me back to a night in college when he sang "American Pie" onstage at a Boston bar, his dreamy blue eyes looking right out at me.

A real wake-up call came a few months after Russ and Michael returned from London, when we learned that a married friend had had an affair. The couple would later divorce. We looked at each other and said, "That's not going to happen to us."

Another one of my mother's sayings is that in a relationship, someone is always chasing and someone is being chased. After our romantic weekend away, I felt a bit soothed, as if I could stop chasing, but I chose not to run away, either, as my husband slowly, subtly, and sweetly began to make more time for our family, for me.

That winter, on Valentine's Day, he and Michael rewrote the lyrics to "Good Riddance," the song Michael sang on graduation day.

Then they sang a duet for me while Michael played the guitar. I cry every time I watch the video, especially when I hear the refrain: "It's something that we should express but don't on many days, we love you more than words will ever say."

Could it be that simple, that my husband just hadn't been expressing his love? That feels too simple. What I believe now is that he didn't fully appreciate me until he saw how well my son had pulled through his crisis; he recognized what I had done for our child and our family. We got thrown a curveball, one that caused me to question myself, my marriage, and my son. But trying to help Michael also gave me a new sense of purpose at a time when I'd lost my identity, going from journalist to full-time mom, which contributed to my frustration.

For many years, I felt that the work I did raising our kids was not valued, by my husband or by me. But as we began talking civilly again (not just during cocktail hour), our relationship got better too. In the three decades we've been married, I can count on one hand the number of times my husband has cried. I have cried far too many times, wasting energy I could have spent enjoying my marriage, my husband, my kids, and my life.

Russ ultimately sold his practice to a hospital, which made his work less stressful and more lucrative. In the past, I hadn't taken responsibility for our family's finances, justifying my spending sprees by saying, "We need to do this for Michael." But once Russ's work situation was sorted out, I began giving some serious thought to my own career and started a business doing college essay tutoring. My income was meager at first, but after five or six years, I would be able to contribute a chunk to the kids' college educations. Making money allowed me some financial freedom, too, which I think is important in a marriage, because feeling dependent affected my behavior and fueled my resentment. When we finally got back on solid ground financially, we sat down together to do some serious financial planning and talked about what we wanted *our* future together to look like.

185

Chapter 20

Leap of Faith

After being quiet all summer, Michael began ticcing again in the fall, probably because he was nervous about starting over at a new high school. But he was ready. Though I drove him to school on the first day, a 30-minute ride, the next day he took the Metro-North commuter train on his own, dressed in the unofficial school uniform of khaki pants, a light-blue oxford, and a tie (Russ had shown him how to knot it the day before).

I eyed the crowd at the station at 7 a.m.: some other boys heading to the same high school, kids heading to other private schools, and lots of commuters. It seemed safe enough, but Michael seemed too young to be traveling alone. Predictably, when the train pulled out of the station, I got choked up. My oldest child was on his way to a new life without me, the train a first step toward creating a healthy boundary, one that would need to stretch even further as he inched toward college.

On his second day, when I picked him up in the afternoon, he said, "Mom, I got a JUG because I was late for class."

"What's a JUG?"

"JUG stands for Justice Under God. That's what they call detention!"

So began ninth grade at the Catholic high school.

We switched him to an earlier train, but I immediately began wondering if I had made a mistake: Were the hippie school and the Catholic school too different? There was no wandering the halls, popping into the music room to jam, or spending hours creating elaborate art projects. No go-carts, but plenty of God. And yes, there were tests and grades.

But I tried to focus on how far he'd come instead of dwelling on everything that might go wrong sending a budding atheist to a Catholic school, and a jock haven at that, where no one knew about his Tourette.

I remember how the middle school math teacher had raised her eyebrows when I told her where Michael was going to high school. "It's a leap of faith," I told her. I had hoped that Michael would adjust and that he might take to Jesuit education as Russ had. Russ felt at home at Boston College even though he wasn't raised Catholic. I convinced myself the Jesuit community would offer a safety net—and a springboard.

But Michael also tried out and was accepted to be a drummer in the jazz band. We took it as a good sign that the band director had a huge Led Zeppelin poster hanging in her office.

Yet I couldn't help but do several things to ease his transition. In August, I sent his guidance counselor an email with information for Michael's teachers, including a link to a few Tourette fact sheets. I wanted to get ahead of the curve, and the cursing, if it returned. I made it clear that Michael preferred that teachers ignore his tics because he did not want to draw attention to himself, and he did not want his new classmates to know he had Tourette. I said he would share this information in due time once he began to make friends.

I also set up a meeting with all of his teachers during the second week of school. I wanted to try to build bridges so we could work as a team in case things went awry. Russ came too. All of his teachers attended, plus his guidance counselor and her boss. They seemed interested, if not overly empathetic, and I was thrilled that so many of them had shown up. But I was also wary, wondering which one would let us down.

It turned out not to be a teacher at all.

In December, his guidance counselor asked if Michael wanted extra time on midterms. He said he did not. He would never again receive an accommodation to compensate for his disability.

As we hit the third anniversary of his diagnosis, Michael was pulling in A's and B's and had no need for the peer tutor (a student who tutored classmates for free) that we had arranged to make sure he stayed on track in math. He moved to honors geometry the following year and got straight A's in math all four years.

"Why do you think you waited all these years to start trying your best in school?" I asked one day.

"I didn't want to waste my energy."

He turned out not to mind going to mandatory mass every month, not to mention third-period prayer daily. One day, when I picked him up from school, he said, "Guess what my theology teacher said? I may have broken a record for the highest score ever on the theology midterm!"

Then, the following spring, he had a setback. In September, he joined the crew team. He was reluctant, but Russ and I urged him on. At 14, Michael was still quite short and stout—not the classic rower's body—but we saw it as a way for an out-of-town kid to make friends.

"Are the kids nice to you?" I asked him nonchalantly one day while driving home in the car. Maybe it was a mother's intuition.

"Yeah."

There was just enough hesitation for me to question his honesty.

A technique I learned in journalism school is that if a source is not forthcoming, try rephrasing the same questions later on in the interview.

"Are some kids not nice?"

"Yeah."

"What do they do?"

"Sometimes they call me names."

"Like what?"

Silence.

I slowed down, but only a little, then made a sharp right turn onto a side street. The car jerked as I put it into park.

"I'm not moving until you tell me. What names do they call you?"

He sat in the passenger seat in his jeans and royal-blue Abercrombie hoodie.

Silence. My son seemed more embarrassed than agitated.

I thought about the past eight months, when Michael was busy with crew and jazz band and seemed happy. As the school year progressed, the only thing he didn't seem to have was a lot of friends, and no good friends.

"They call me fat. Idiot. Gay." He didn't look at me as he said it.

Hearing this blindsided me.

"Is it one kid or several?"

"There are three of them, but one kid is the worst."

"Does he ever hurt you?"

"He punches me sometimes, really hard in the arm. But he pretends he's joking."

Michael said it happened on the bus they took to and from the boathouse from school, about a 20-minute ride each way.

"Does he ever do it in front of the other boys?"

"He only does it in front of other kids. That's the point."

"When did it start?"

"In the fall. And it's getting worse."

I unbuckled and tried to reach over to hug him, but he recoiled. I placed my hand on his hand instead. Then I put the car in gear and drove home. I had work to do, or so I thought.

Later, he confessed that he hadn't told me because he was afraid I would go all mama bear fighting for her cub. Still, I emailed the guidance counselor, copying the coach and the head of discipline (the guy who handed out the JUGs). I tried to be levelheaded, like Russ, and not an overbearing helicopter mom. The head of guidance met with Michael the next day, during his free period. I was not invited to the meeting, which surprised me.

Afterward, the head of guidance called the three boys in and spoke to them privately. The boys' parents were not told, and no disciplinary action was taken, but the guidance counselor assured me that the talking-to would stop the behavior.

I had expected the JUG-dispensing disciplinarian to show up with a wooden paddle, as the nuns did back in the day, or at least the modern equivalent. But I decided to trust the school administrators. They had raised more boys to men than I had.

But the bullying persisted, so I requested an in-person meeting with the guidance counselor, a veteran educator whom I had come to trust. Russ did not come with me, and I didn't ask him to attend. I could handle this, and somehow, I remained calm, mostly because I was afraid I'd embarrass Michael. I also didn't want the administration to write me off. Which by now I knew was not entirely hyperbole.

Since there were only four days left of school, I agreed when the guidance counselor suggested that we wait it out, reminding myself that Michael hadn't even wanted to report the behavior, but I had insisted.

Uncharacteristically, I tried to focus on the big picture: Michael's Tourette was largely under control with the medicine. He still ticced at home, sometimes frequently. But he finished freshman year without one fellow student uncovering his secret. Still, I wished he felt confident enough or had made good enough friends to come clean. I also wanted him to stand up for himself and to have a friend group. I wanted him to do a lot, given that he was only a freshman in high school.

~

Michael stayed on the crew team through the fall of sophomore year, then told us he didn't want to try out in the spring. Russ and I agreed, as long as he joined some clubs and worked out to stay in shape.

Like many parents, we discouraged our kids from quitting, but this move was a good one. During the winter, Michael saw a friend who is a nutritionist, who taught him how to eat a protein-packed diet as a pescatarian (he had begun to eat seafood after two years as a vegetarian). Within a few months, he lost his extra weight and grew three inches, his round, baby face hollowing and his voice deepening. He could barely hit the high notes in his latest School of Rock show, Tom Petty.

Since he was not ticcing much, we also weaned Michael off all of his medications by Christmas of his sophomore year, which was a huge relief after four years and may have accelerated his weight loss. Even more astonishing to me was that Michael found interests and clubs he enjoyed, from Model UN to the school's political magazine, where he started as a writer and would become the editor-in-chief as a junior. He thrived in these extracurricular clubs, formed his friend group, and found another passion, politics. He also launched his own blog—for fun—called Polititurk. Soon, Michael's passion for music was matched by his love of politics and international affairs.

The summer between freshman and sophomore year, he had volunteered to work on the campaign for our local congressman's reelection. I'll admit, it was my idea; he was having trouble finding a paying summer job aside from a few dog-walking gigs in the neighborhood. But calling voters and canvassing in neighborhoods all over the county turned out to be a good job for a boy once afraid to leave the house. He grew to love talking with adults about current events and politics and became passionate about world affairs.

As part of his school's service requirement, he also began teaching drums and guitar every week to at-risk students at an elementary school in Bridgeport, a volunteer activity he would continue throughout high school. I loved that music had helped him get through difficult times and that he was now giving back to help kids who didn't have the resources to pay for private music lessons.

Witnessing all of this was heartwarming. Michael was not the butterfly who sprang fully formed from a chrysalis or the scrawny weakling who became a buff bodybuilder. His change was slow, like a tree that doesn't bear fruit for years and is suddenly laden with apples. Of course, it helped that the bullies were no longer bothering him.

These newfound passions, plus his continued affinity for music, helped him develop the confidence to tell people the secret he had hidden since he was in sixth grade. It happened in the spring of his junior year, when his AP Spanish teacher assigned the class the essay topic "Who am I?" At first, Michael didn't want to write about Tourette because he would have to present it in front of the class. But after reading the first drafts, the teacher told the class to "go deeper." Michael told me all of this as I was making dinner one night, then he said, "I'm going to write the second paper on having Tourette."

"That's wonderful."

"I need to get my grade up in this class," he said.

I'd like to think he chose to divulge his biggest secret for more noble reasons, but he was upset that his midterm grade was a B.

"Are you nervous?"

"Yes!" he said.

Then he became quiet and got an awkward look on his face.

"Mom, Tourette syndrome is the butt of jokes at school."

"Your Tourette?" I asked, confused.

"No, just people with Tourette. Kids see it in movies and make fun of it."

Michael would be reading out loud to teenage boys who poked fun at the condition after seeing a character with Tourette on TV or hearing comedians joke about it. All the shit-talk. But by then, I knew he could handle it. Like me, he had grown some armor.

I had waited for this moment for years, but when it finally happened, it caught me off guard. He had been on a few class trips, shared hotel rooms with classmates, and spent countless hours at the local pizza place with his friends—yes, he had made several. He also went on a school retreat billed as a time for "prayer, reflection, friendship, and community." He never used any of these opportunities to share his secret with boys he had known for three years. Even his closest friends had no idea.

Five years and four months, 300 weeks, and nearly 2,000 days since that day when Michael sat on our couch shouting obscenities, he was able to tell the people in his world, *I have Tourette syndrome.*

That's a long time to keep a secret.

Later that night, he showed me his essay.

> *This affliction drastically changed my life in that it made me very self-conscious about myself, and it made me afraid to meet new people and step out of my comfort zone due to a fear of what they would think of me. Ever since this time, I have felt like I had to show people that I was more than what I had been in the past.*

In other words, he had something to prove.

It took me a long time to admit that I did too.

193

The whole experience made me think back to what I wanted for my kids when they were babies. Good teeth and a good education were not enough.

I am blessed to have been raised in a small, safe town by a large, loving family. But because of where I came from, and the early education I didn't get, I often felt less intelligent, less sophisticated, and less educated—even after I earned my B.A. and a master's degree. That "less than" feeling takes a long time to go away.

Maybe that's one reason why, for so long, I had defined myself by my shortcomings. I wasn't the cool mom. I wasn't the skinny, Lululemon-wearing, SoulCycle-junkie mom. I wasn't the stylish, Jimmy Choo shoe–wearing mom. I wasn't the mom who made a homemade meal every night. I wasn't the mom whose house was perfectly decorated—or neat and organized. I wasn't the mom who earned six figures. I wasn't the übervolunteer, head-of-the-PTA mom.

Instead, I learned that being a mom—and life—is not totally under my control. Just as Michael couldn't control his cursing, I can't control what Michael says or does or who he chooses to become. All I can control is myself, and it took loosening my hold a bit to begin to figure out who I was, outside of my kids and my marriage. Rather than feeling less than, I am grateful I could become the person and mother I ended up being, evolving and growing through midlife in ways I never would have if I had made different choices. I also realize now, more than ever, what a luxury it was to have had those choices. And I am grateful for that privilege.

I'm proud I defied the odds I set for myself by becoming an expert on Michael's condition, finding treatments and people who could help; making sure he got a good education; and helping him navigate the landmines of middle and high school. I was his champion and protector, for years. But it took much longer for me to realize all that Michael did for me.

194

Michael has also learned to define himself differently. I started out feeling I was the only one who could solve his problems. Sure, the medicine went a long way toward tamping down Michael's tics, but in the end, he was still a teenager who had to grow up, buckle down at school, and become responsible and accountable for his actions. And he rose to the top, not in spite of but *because* of Tourette, which provided the impetus for him to overcome his insecurities, self-doubt, and self-loathing.

Not long ago, the subject came up about what he was like as a toddler. I called him a terror.

"Really?"

"You don't remember what you were like?" I asked, furrowing my brow in astonishment.

It was an "aha" moment.

I said to him, "You can't remember and I can't forget."

Sometimes I stop and remember what he was like, and I can't help but pray—a "thank you, Lord, we made it through" kind of prayer.

This is the boy who had failed at school.

This is the boy who had almost gotten arrested.

This is the boy who had told me he was a freak.

This is a boy who may have seemed cursed, but he became a blessing to me, and our family.

Epilogue

Thirteen years after our first visit to Yale, researchers there are still searching for the genes that cause Tourette (Michael, Russ, and I all enrolled in a recent study). Many questions remain, but what scientists do know is that there is likely no single Tourette gene; instead, Tourette is what's known as a genetically heterogeneous condition. Dr. Coffman put it to me this way: "We now understand that a change in one gene gives you a little bit of a risk factor to develop Tourette, a change in another gives you another little risk factor to give you Tourette, and it takes a bunch of different genes with different changes to reach a genetic load, where there are enough genetic differences, in a bunch of risk-factor genes, to give that individual Tourette."

I still have questions of my own, but "What makes him tic?" no longer haunts me. Writing about parenting a child with Tourette has given me some much-needed perspective. I am so proud of how both Michael and Katie have turned out, but I bristle when people say things like, "It all worked out." It didn't all work out. I did a lot of work to parent my children and teach them values that oftentimes went against the grain. I hope that both of my children—and my husband (yes, we are still married)—will look back on my helpful hints and worrywart tendencies and see them as a form of love. Because that is the only way I know how to parent.

During the latter part of Michael's high school years, my role wavered between being a warrior who felt the need to protect Michael and letting him live his life. As much as I hovered, I tried to be less protective than my parents were with me. I relished those last couple of years, with both children at home, and jumped at every chance to spend time together one-to-one and as a family.

Despite being back at work for a decade as a writer and tutor, I still sometimes struggle to find purpose in my days, now that my kids have both left home; but I've begun taking better care of my mind and body. Case in point: I am finally able to watch the Australian lady meditate on YouTube, and I do her five-minute meditation every morning.

When I look back at all of the challenges, I wonder if this is what I was preparing for my whole life. But I didn't do anything many mothers with a kid with a medical or learning disability hadn't done for their children.

As for Michael, in the spring of his senior year, he was admitted to his dream college: Georgetown University. By the time he stepped foot on campus, he was mature, responsible, self-aware, and excited to figure out who he could become. After we dropped him off at college, I did my best to give him a wide berth and rarely called or even texted at first. By the second semester, after I had given him some space, he began calling me almost daily just to chat.

Once Michael left for college, we had Katie at home for two years, and Russ and I enjoyed giving her more attention and time (though the feeling was not always mutual). Katie pulled her head out of her books and became a rower in eighth grade. In high school, she proved to be one of those competitive kids—she won multiple medals as a lightweight rower, including a national championship.

Soon after she graduated from the University of Virginia in 2023, the two of us were musing about where that drive came from, and she told me that part of it had to do with growing up with a brother who had Tourette, and from trying to be the "good" child. I get that. My daughter's physical strength is obvious to the naked eye, but what you can't see may be even more formidable. Being the "typical" child who lived through some stormy times has made her wise beyond her years, with a steely, calm reserve. She has told me that it's easy to forget how much a part of Michael's life and our lives his Tourette was, and it certainly broadened her perspective. "I went from a 9-year-old thinking he was faking it to defending him when my friends came over," she recalled. "It made me a more empathic and accepting person."

After Michael graduated from college in 2021, he announced that he wanted to pursue a career in the restaurant and food industry (he is half-Italian, after all). Almost three years in, he works as a chef in a restaurant in Los Angeles and runs pop-up restaurants that focus on raw, plant-based ingredients with his girlfriend (despite his fears, he has had a few). And though he can no longer sing the high notes in Led Zeppelin songs, music still grounds him and allows him to escape. When he plays drums, he doesn't have a care in the world.

Michael's move to California was bittersweet. I always knew that separating would be hard. For me. But he had been preparing to take flight for years. When I dropped him off at the airport, I gave him a hug, reached up to cup his face in my hands, and tried to hold back my tears. But as always, he could read me, and as he looked back down at me, he smiled and said, "Mom, you're gonna be OK."

And I was. I am. One thing that is clear to me now is that I didn't have to be the hero of this story.

In some ways, Michael was the hero. In the end, maybe he helped heal himself. He rarely tics these days, and few people know he has Tourette. But even if he did tic, he would brush it off. He may have Tourette, but Tourette definitely doesn't have him.

Acknowledgments

I started writing this book by scribbling notes to myself because I couldn't believe what was happening to my son and my family. It took a decade to figure out how to tell our story in a way that might be helpful to parents of children with Tourette syndrome and other kids who are neurodivergent.

There are so many people who helped me write a happy ending to this story—one I couldn't have imagined a decade ago.

What Makes Him Tic? would not be published without the editors and agents who developed and honed the manuscript or read bits and pieces of related work: Linda Carbone, Gary Krebs, Cherise Fisher, Sue Shapiro, and Samantha Shanley at GrubStreet in Boston. Thank you also to my friends and colleagues who read and weighed in on the manuscript: Sarah Rosell, Deborah Rimmler, Daisy Florin, and Lynn Prowitt.

To the early believers: Marilyn Allen, Tessa Smith McGovern, and especially Carol Dannhauser of the Fairfield County Story Lab, where I spent many hours typing in solitude. And a shout-out to everyone in my original writing class at the Westport Writers' Workshop, especially Marcelle Soviero, who helped me evolve from a journalist into a memoirist.

I am grateful to David LeGere and Miranda Heyman at Woodhall Press for acquiring the book, answering my endless questions leading up to publication, and nudging me across the finish line. To others who had a hand in the publication: Ryan Fox, LJ Mucci, Jessica Dionne, Natalia Olbinski, Kiana Stockwell, and my publicist (and simpatico parent) Laura Rossi. And my heartfelt thanks to all of the troubleshooters who tolerated my last-minute madness and came to my rescue: Ilana Krebs, Gabi Coatsworth, and Marli Higa, whose 11th-hour edits were invaluable.

Last but not least, an enormous thank you to my friend and editor extraordinaire, Paula Derrow, who helped shape the story, polished my prose and did so much more to help me publish a book I am proud of.

For any helpers I forgot, please accept my apologies—I will buy you a bourbon at the book launch!

To the educators and teachers who supported and mentored Michael and guided him on his journey from boy to man: Shelley Somers, Arona Smotrich, Joy Lenters, Jeremy Grob, Christine Evans, Jason Mis, John Szablewicz, Melissa Laguzza, and especially, John Hanrahan. And a huge thank you to Tony Mullen, whose words of wisdom still guide me. To Steve Kennedy, Byl Cote, and Carl Goding of the School of Rock, where Michael found a second home—you guys rock!

I am incredibly grateful for Michael's medical team, who also acted as invaluable resources as I researched Tourette syndrome: Kevin Kalikow, MD; Denis Sukhodolsky, Ph.D.; and Dorothy Levine, M.D. In particular, Russ and I are indebted to Robert King, M.D., whose intellect is matched only by his humanity.

Thank you to the other distinguished medical experts I interviewed who were so generous with their time: Keith Coffman, MD, James Leckman, M.D., John Walkup, M.D., and Graham Hartke, Psy.D.

A big thanks to other caring folks who helped me help Michael: Jacques Depardieu, Francesco Bibbiani, M.D., Richelle Jones, Carol Macleod, Kimberly DuBois, Dawn Denberg, Anitra Brooks, Fayne Molloy, Amy Zabin, and Jane Ross and the Smart Kids with Learning Disabilities community.

And a huge thanks to the Tourette Association of America (TAA), especially Amanda Talty, Helene Walisever, James Saracini, and Emma O'Connell, and the entire team that works to remove the stigma surrounding Tourette, fund research, and support children and adults with Tourette. From the very beginning when I received brochures, to the lectures and webinars I attended and the interviews with experts affiliated with the TAA, the organization has been an invaluable resource.

To my readers, particularly those in the Tourette community, I hope you find information, hope, and comfort in these pages.

Finally, I am lucky to have a big, caring group of friends who accepted and loved Michael and helped me, whether it was through moral support or simply by checking in: Laura Dahm, the 'hood mamas (and their kids)—Claire Muldoon and Jody Ellsworth—the Hail Marys (my Boston College besties), Tony Cammarota, Marian Marino Lucier, Cheryl and Chip Skowron, and Scotty and Craig Reiss.

And of course, my family, especially my sister Mindy McKeown, sisters-in-law Joanne Pullia and Laura Graff, Liz and Charlie Turk, Frank Copsidas, Fr. Frank Donio, S.A.C., and my mother-in-law, Helga, who just kept on showing up to help. And to my mother, who called me every day and prayed for Michael. It meant the world to hear her say I did a good job raising him through this challenge.

To Russ, thank you for finally seeing things my way. Just kidding. Thanks for being my rock—and countering my motherhood angst with your glass-half-full outlook on life. I'll take a refill, please.

To both of the young Turks, it has been my great honor in life to be your mother.

To my sweet and kind Katie, who never complained and brings us such great joy with her wit and wisdom. I know all of this wasn't easy for you, but you never cease to amaze and inspire me.

Finally, to Michael, thank you for trusting me to tell your story. You taught me more than I could ever teach you.

About the Author

Michele Turk has worked as a journalist for three decades, covering parenting, health, and education. Her articles and essays have appeared in *Bloomberg Businessweek, Parents, Parenting, the Hartford Courant, Elle, USA Weekend, The Washington Post, Brain, Child,* and *Next Avenue.* She has served as president of the Connecticut Press Club since 2015. Turk lives with her husband, Russ, in Fairfield County, Connecticut.

Notes

Chapter 1

1. I learned that Tourette: No author. "Data & Statistics on Tourette Syndrome". *Centers For Disease Control and Prevention.* May 4, 2023. https://www.cdc.gov/ncbddd/tourette/data.html.
2. and less common in Hispanic and Black people: No author. "Prevalence of Diagnosed Tourette Syndrome in Persons aged 6-17 years–United States, 2007". *MMWR Morb Mortal Wkly.* Rep. June 5, 2009. 58(21):581-5. https://pubmed.ncbi.nlm.nih.gov/19498335/.
3. It surprised me to learn that this symptom was exceedingly rare,": No author. "Five Things You May Not Know About Tourette Syndrome". *Centers For Disease Control and Prevention.* Last reviewed May 3, 2023. https://www.cdc.gov/ncbddd/tourette/features/tourette-five-things.html.
4. "Probably the most common misbelief about Tourette, often seen on TV and in movies": No author. "Five Things You May Not Know About Tourette Syndrome". *Centers For Disease Control and Prevention.* Last reviewed May 3, 2023. https://www.cdc.gov/ncbddd/tourette/features/tourette-five-things.html.

Chapter 2

1. Two years before I had Michael, I published an essay: Michele Pullia Turk. "Motherhood Angst". Washington Post. September 11, 1997. https://www.washingtonpost.com/archive/lifestyle/1997/09/11/motherhood-angst/1665c9bb-b688-49be-af1f-fa4dd732c6a3/.

Chapter 3

1. I had read that PANDAS: No author. "PANDAS—Questions and Answers". *National Institutes of Health.* Revised 2019. https://www.nimh.nih.gov/health/publications/pandas#:~:text=PANDAS%20is%20short%20for%20Pediatric,strep%20throat%20or%20scarlet%20fever.

2. French neurologist Georges Gilles de la Tourette is credited: F Gilson. "Gilles de la Tourette: de geschiedenis van de man en zijn ziekte" [Gilles de la Tourette: The history of the man and his illness; a medical historical study]. *Tijdschr Psychiatr.* 2012. 54(8):770. https://pubmed.ncbi.nlm. nih.gov/22811054/#:~:text=Results%3A%20In%201885%20Gilles%20 de,de%20Gilles%20de%20la%20Tourette.

3. Scientists no longer view it that way: '[Tourette] has long rested in the shadowy borderland between neurology and psychiatry': Janice R Stevens and Paul Blachly. "Successful Treatment of the Maladie des Tics: Gilles de la Tourette's Syndrome". 112 (6): 541–545 doi:10.1001/ archpedi.1966.02090150085006. December 1966. https://jamanetwork. com/journals/jamapediatrics/article-abstract/502013.

4. In fact, the Tourette Association of America (TAA), was not founded until the 1970s: No author. "Mission & History". *Tourette Association of America.* No published date. https://tourette.org/about-us/mission- and-history/#:~:text=Founded%20in%201972%2C%20the%20 Tourette,Tourette%20Syndrome%20and%20Tic%20Disorders.

5. There was a memorable scene from Season 3 of the show "Curb Your Enthusiasm,": James Sheehan. "Tourettes Outburst in Restaurant". YouTube Video. 1:43. June 29, 2010. https://tinyurl.com/nhyazk6y.

6. In my research, I came across a video: OWN. "The 2nd Grade Teacher with Tourette Syndrome The Oprah Winfrey Show". YouTube Video. 7:04. March 5, 2020. https://www.youtube.com/watch?v=WTtwmyyUwSY.

7. "The media in our country": Keith Coffman. Interviewed by author. Zoom. March 8, 2023.

8. Even the name of the condition has changed: "Diagnostic and Statistical Manual of Mental Disorders". *American Psychiatric Association.* Amer Psychiatric Pub Inc. 5th edition. March 16, 2022. https://tinyurl. com/2p82yjec.

9. One statistic that gave me a glimmer of hope: Dr. James Leckman. Lecture at Greenwich Hospital. June 9, 2011.

10. Iceberg illustration poster. There was an image that kept popping up: No author. "Iceberg Illustration Poster". *Tourette Association of America.* No published date. https://tourette.org/resource/iceberg-illustration-poster/.

11. The blame game comes as no surprise: Dr. James Leckman. Interviewed by author. Zoom. March 7, 2023.

12. According to a book I picked up early on, *A Family's Guide to Tourette Syndrome,* Edited by John T. Walkup, Jonathan W. Mink, and Kevin St. P. McNaught. iUniverse. 2012.

13. I hadn't thought of that much until the night: "HBO and the Tourette Syndrome Association present "I Have Tourette's But Tourette's Doesn't Have Me". HBO Family. 2005 Home Box Office Inc and Tourette Syndrome Association Inc.

Chapter 4

1. Back then, medical residents in New York City still worked up to 120 hours a week: Marc K. Wallack and Lynn Chao. "Resident Work Hours: The Evolution of a Revolution". *Arch Surg.* 136(12):1426–1432. Published October 2001. https://jamanetwork.com/journals/jamasurgery/fullarticle/392566.

2. A study conducted two years after we were married: Tarayn Grizzard. "Love in the Time of Medical School". *American Family Physician.* September 1, 2002. https://www.aafp.org/pubs/afp/issues/2002/0901/p907.html.

3. Yale is now one of 21 Centers of Excellence: No author. "Centers of Excellence Locations." *Tourette Association of America.* No date. https://tourette.org/about-tourette/overview/centers-of-excellence/center-excellence-locations/.

4. Incidence of coprophenomena: Fortunately, only a minority of individuals: Roger D Freeman et al. "Coprophenomena in Tourette syndrome". *Developmental medicine and child neurology* vol. 51, 3. March 2009. 218-27. https://pubmed.ncbi.nlm.nih.gov/19183216/.

5. It is true that cursing can occur: *Musicophilia: Tales of Music and the Brain.* Oliver Sacks. Knopf Books. October 16, 2007. https://www.amazon.com/Musicophilia-Tales-Music-Oliver-Sacks/dp/1400040817/ref=tmm_hrd_swatch_0?_encoding=UTF8&qid=1696365889&sr=8-1.

6. In 2021, the TAA ran an awareness campaign: Tourette Association of America. "Dropping F(act)-Bombs". Facebook. November 30, 2021. https://www.facebook.com/TouretteAssociation/.videos/437316681120366/. Amanda Talty (TAA president). Interviewed by author. Zoom. March 13, 2023.

Chapter 5

1. Yet when his preschool teacher recommended I read a book called *Your Defiant Child: Eight Steps to Better Behavior:* Russell A. Barkley and Christine M. Benton. The Guilford Press. 2nd Edition. July 2, 2013. https://tinyurl.com/yvr5szx.
2. Later I would turn to books: *Jump-Starting Boys:* Pam Withers and Cynthia Gill. Simon & Schuster. July 13, 2013. *Driven to Distraction.* Edward M Hallowell and John J Ratey. Anchor. September 13, 2011.

Chapter 6

1. *The New York Times* writer: "There was an undercurrent of competitiveness to everything," Joanne Kaufman. "A Historical Novelist's Decorating Scheme: 'Books and Dog Hair'". *The New York Times.* June 9, 2020. https://www.nytimes.com/2020/06/09/realestate/novelist-beatriz-williams-at-home-decor.html.
2. According to a Tourette Association's "impact survey": No author. "Impact Survey". *Tourette Association of America.* No published date. https://tourette.org/research-medical/impact-survey/.
3. Helene Walisever, a clinical psychologist: Helene Walisever. Interviewed by author. Zoom. February 22, 2023.
4. The number of people with a tic disorder: Dr. John Walkup. Interviewed by author. Zoom. March 28, 2023.
5. The CDC monitors the prevalence: No author. "The National Survey of Children's Health". No date. https://www.childhealthdata.org/learn-about-the-nsch/NSCH.
6. One 2020 study summed up the conundrum this way: Mary F Seideman and Travis A Seideman. "A Review of the Current Treatment of Tourette Syndrome". *The journal of pediatric pharmacology and therapeutics: JPPT* vol. 25. 5 401-412, 2020. doi:10.5863/1551-6776-25.5.401. https://www.ncbi.nlm.nih.gov/pmc/articles/PMC7337131/.

Chapter 7

1. And I'd also gotten an appointment with a psychiatrist: Dr. Kevin Kalikow. Doctor visit. In person. January 2011.

2. Dr. Kalikow was the author: Kevin T. Kalikow. *Your Child in the Balance.* Vanguard Pr. January 1, 2006. https://tinyurl.com/2p8ypnac.

3. and he later published a second book: *Kids on Meds: Up-to-Date Information About the Most Commonly Prescribed Psychiatric Medications:* Kevin T. Kalikow. W.W. Norton & Company. September 12, 2011. https://tinyurl.com/4af4d7wx.

4. a sensation or feeling that needs to be satisfied: J F Leckman, D E Walker, and D J Cohen. "Premonitory urges in Tourette's syndrome". *The American Journal of Psychiatry.* vol. 150 1. January 1993. 98-102. doi:10.1176/ajp.150.1.98. https://pubmed.ncbi.nlm.nih.gov/8417589/.

5. Dr. King reminded me: Dr. Robert King. Doctor visit. In person. February 2, 2011.

Chapter 8

1. Emotional overload can occur: No author. "Emotional Overload: Understanding Non-Tic Related Behaviors in Tourette Syndrome". *Tourette Association of America.* No date. https://tourette.org/wp-content/uploads/TAA-GuideEmotionalOverloadWEB.pdf.

2. Michael's main source of excitement was watching *American Idol*. ABC. https://abc.com/shows/american-idol/.

Chapter 9

1. When we arrived at Dr. Sukhodolsky's office at Yale: Denis Sukhodolsky, ph.D. Doctor visit. In person. January 2011.

2. CBIT would become an effective first-line treatment: Simon Morand-Beaulieu, Michael J. Crowley, Heidi Grantz, James F. Leckman, Lawrence Scahill, and Denis G. Sukhodolsky. *International Federation of Clinical Neurophysiology.* https://doi.org/10.1016/j.clinph.2022.07.5001388-2457/ 2022. Published by Elsevier B.V. July 17, 2022.

3. Simon Morand-Beaulieu, Michael J. Crowley, Heidi Grantz1, James F. Leckman, Denis G. Sukhodolsky. "Functional connectivity during tic suppression predicts reductions in vocal tics following behavior therapy in children with Tourette syndrome". *Psychological Medicine* 1–8. June 6, 2023. https://doi.org/10.1017/S0033291723001940.

4. In 2010, a large, multi-center study was published: John Piacentini, Douglas W. Woods, and Lawrence Scahill. "Behavior Therapy for Children With Tourette Disorder: A Randomized Controlled Trial". *JAMA*, Republished in 2010. 303(19): originally published in 1929–1937. doi:10.1001/jama.2010.607. https://jamanetwork.com/journals/jama/fullarticle/185896.

5. The Rutgers University Tourette Clinic witnessed a 97% increase: Sponsored by the NJ Center for Tourette Syndrome & Associated Disorders (NJCTS). Graham Hartke. "Understanding and Responding to Sudden Onset Tics in Teens". Webinar. February 23, 2022.

6. According to the book *Natural Treatments for Tics and Tourette's: A Patient and Family Guide:* Sheila Rogers DeMare. North Atlantic Books. October 21, 2008. https://tinyurl.com/mpvxakbm.

7. A few years later. Sheila Rogers DeMare. "Why The Tourette Association Of America Should Be Investigated Part 1". *Latitudes.* March 23, 2014. https://latitudes.org/tourette-syndrome-association-should-be-investigated/.

8. By 2022, *Tourette Syndrome:* Davide Martino and James F Leckman, 2nd Edition. Oxford University Press. June 14, 2022. https://tinyurl.com/5b8v2zs8.

9. study that showed improvement in Tourette patients: No author. "A New Use for Marijuana". *The New York Times.* March 31, 2010. https://archive.nytimes.com/consults.blogs.nytimes.com/2010/03/31/a-new-use-for-medical-marijuana/.

10. "good-enough mother" — the term British pediatrician: "Good enough is good enough!". Charlotte Sidebotham. *The British Journal of General Practice: the Journal of the Royal College of General Practitioners.* vol. 67,660. 311. July 2017. doi:10.3399/bjgp17X691409. https://www.ncbi.nlm.nih.gov/pmc/articles/PMC5565862/.

11. a promising study: LM Pelsser, K Frankena, and J Toorman et al. "Effects of a restricted elimination diet on the behaviour of children with attention-deficit hyperactivity disorder (INCA study): a randomised controlled trial". *Lancet.* May 7, 2011. 377: 494-503. https://doi.org/10.1016/S0140-6736(11)60632-6. https://www.thelancet.com/journals/lancet/article/PIIS0140-6736(11)60632-6/fulltext.

Chapter 10

1. The FDA approved Risperdal in 1993: Shawn E McNeil, Jonathan R Gibbons, and Mark Cogburn. "Risperidone". Updated January 16, 2023. *StatPearls*. StatPearls Publishing. https://www.ncbi.nlm.nih.gov/books/NBK459313/.
2. Kevin T. Kalikow. *Your Child in the Balance*. Vanguard Pr. January 1, 2006. https://tinyurl.com/2p8ypnac.

Chapter 11

1. A 504 Plan refers to: No author. "Section 504, Rehabilitation Act of 1973". U.S. Department of Labor. No date. https://www.dol.gov/agencies/oasam/centers-offices/civil-rights-center/statutes/section-504-rehabilitation-act-of-1973.
2. I later learned that 34 percent of kids: No author. "Data and Statistics on Tourette Syndrome". *Center for Disease Control and Prevention*. Reviewed May 4, 2023. https://www.cdc.gov/ncbddd/tourette/data.html.
3. And in the 2020/21 TAA impact survey: No author. "The National Survey of Children's Health". No date. https://www.childhealthdata.org/learn-about-the-nsch/NSCH.
4. a 2007 episode of *South Park* titled "Le Petit Tourette:" No author. "Le Petit Tourette." South Park website. No date. https://southpark.cc.com/wiki/Le_Petit_Tourette.
5. After *The Simpsons* aired a segment: Mary Elizabeth Cronin. "Tourette's Isn't Funny, Bart Simpson — Renton Boy Seeks Network Apology". *Seattle Times*. February 1, 1993. https://archive.seattletimes.com/archive/?date=19930201&slug=1683046.
6. In one Canadian study that reviewed fictional films and TV shows, Samantha Calder-Sprackman, Stephanie Sutherland, and Asif Doja. "The Portrayal of Tourette Syndrome in Film and Television". *The Canadian Journal of Neurological Sciences Inc.* 41, no. 2 (2014): 226–32. doi:10.1017/S0317167100016620. September 23, 2014. https://www.cambridge.org/core/services/aop-cambridge-core/content/view/S0317167100016620.
7. in 2018, when Grammy-award winner Billie Eilish: Nicole Engelman. "Billie Eilish Reveals She Has Tourette Syndrome After Compilation of Her Tics Emerges Online". *Billboard*.

November 27, 2018. https://www.billboard.com/music/pop/
billie-eilish-tourette-syndrome-diagnosis-8486878/.

8. Toward the end of the book, the teacher takes the class to a junkyard:
Patricia Polacco. *The Junkyard Wonders*. Philomel Books. July 8, 2010.

Chapter 12

1. until I read the best-selling book, *Quiet,* by Susan Cain. Crown. January 24,
2012.

2. In 1997 I bought a book called *It's about Time: The 6 Styles of
Procrastination and How to Overcome Them:* Linda Sapadin and Jack
Maguire. Penguin Books. June 1, 1997. https://tinyurl.com/yjrn87aj.

3. Students with disabilities are two to three times: No author. "5
Important Facts". No date. *Pacer.* https://www.pacer.org/bullying/info/
students-with-disabilities/.

4. According to the most recent TAA impact survey: No author.
"The National Survey of Children's Health". No date. https://www.
childhealthdata.org/learn-about-the-nsch/NSCH.

5. An Indiana college student was kicked off: Rhonda Wheeler. "Petition
created for student removed off campus due to Tourette syndrome". *The
Shield.* October 12, 2020. https://usishield.com/33380/news/petition-
created-for-student-removed-off-campus-due-to-tourette-syndrome/.

6. A 15-year-old ticcing teenager was asked to leave: Rozina Sini. "Tourette's
teen leaves cinema after complaints she was too noisy". *BBC News.* March
9, 2019. https://www.bbc.com/news/48180926.

7. Many people have been fired: No author. "Americans with Disabilities Act
(ADA)". *Tourette Association of America. No date.* https://tourette.org/
resource/americans-disabilities-act-ada/.

8. School of Rock was launched: No author. "School of Rock Company".
School of Rock. No date. https://www.schoolofrock.com/
company?labelSource=Promotional_Partner.

Chapter 13

1. And walked into a lecture: Barbara Allen-Lyall. No title. Lecture. No
location. February 24, 2012.

2. I remember sitting on my bed, looking at: *Raising Cain: Protecting the
Emotional Life of Boys.* Dan Kindlon and Michael Thompson.

210

Chapter 14

1. The late neurologist Oliver Sacks, author of the best-seller turned movie *Awakenings:* Summit Books. January 1, 1987. https://www.amazon.com/Awakenings-Oliver-W-Sacks/dp/0671648349/ref=tmm_hrd_swatch_0?_encoding=UTF8&qid=1696882620&sr=1-1.
2. also wrote a book entitled *Musicophilia: Tales of Music and the Brain.* Oliver Sacks. Knopf Books. October 16, 2007. https://www.amazon.com/Musicophilia-Tales-Music-Oliver-Sacks/dp/1400040817/ref=tmm_hrd_swatch_0?_encoding=UTF8&qid=1696365889&sr=8-1.
3. "When I'm moving around, I'm not even ticcing: Edward Segarra. "Billie Eilish says she's 'incredibly offended' by people who laugh at her Tourette's syndrome tics". *USA Today.* May 22, 2022. https://www.usatoday.com/story/entertainment/celebrities/2022/05/22/billie-eilish-discusses-tourettes-syndrome-david-letterman-netflix-interview/9887060002/.
4. to the music we played in the car: Music for Little People. All You Need is Love: Beatles Songs for Kids.
5. Tim Howard, known for his dramatic saves: Matthias Fiedler. "US Goalie Tim Howard on Life with Tourette's". *Spiegel International.* May 31, 2013. https://www.spiegel.de/international/world/us-soccer-goalie-tim-howard-speaks-about-tourette-syndrome-a-902729.html.

Chapter 15

1. As Anne Lamott wrote in her book, *Help, Thanks, Wow.* Riverhead Books. November 13, 2012. https://tinyurl.com/5f8pjdba.

Chapter 16

1. In April, I'd traveled to D.C.: Tourette Association Conference. Arlington, VA. April 19, 2012.
2. Since Dr. Walkup's lecture: Matthew E Hirschtritt et al. "Lifetime prevalence, age of risk, and etiology of comorbid psychiatric disorders in Tourette syndrome." *JAMA psychiatry* vol. 72, 4. April 1, 2015. 325-33. doi:10.1001/jamapsychiatry.2014.2650. https://www.ncbi.nlm.nih.gov/pmc/articles/PMC4446055/.

3. In fact, when the TAA surveyed: No author. "Impact Survey". *Tourette Association of America*. No published date. https://tourette.org/research-medical/impact-survey/.

4. In 2022, there was another big change: Amanda Talty (TAA president). Interviewed by author. Zoom. March 13, 2023.

5. After looking at previously published review articles: Sarah C. Tinker, Rebecca H. Bitsko, Melissa L. Danielson, Kimberly Newsome, and Jennifer W. Kaminski. "Estimating the number of people with Tourette syndrome and persistent tic disorder in the United States". Published by Elsevier B.V. Received January 7, 2022; Received in revised form June 2, 2022; Accepted June 13, 2022. https://doi.org/10.1016/j.psychres.2022.114684.

Chapter 18

1. He became a vegetarian after: No author. "'Glass Walls' with Paul McCartney (VIDEO)". *PETA*. No date. https://www.peta.org/videos/glass-walls-2/.